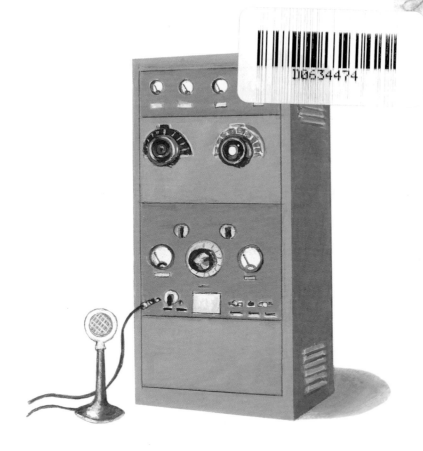

This is a ham radio.

The basic equipment every ham uses are a receiver and a transmitter.

These are usually combined into one device called a transceiver and connected to a separate power supply unit, an antenna, a speaker, and a microphone.

However, most hams don't stick to the basics and their shacks are full of peripheral gear.

These are hams.

Hams come in all shapes and sizes and live all over the world. This book is about a particular ham named Jerry Powell. Jerry was an avid ham radio operator from 1928 until his death in 2000.

He was born in rural Kansas, then became an aerospace engineer and lived in Hackensack, New Jersey with his wife and two sons.

This is a call.

"CQ CQ CQ, this is W2OJW, calling CQ. Whiskey Two
Oscar Juliet Whiskey in Hackensack, New Jersey standing
by for a call..."

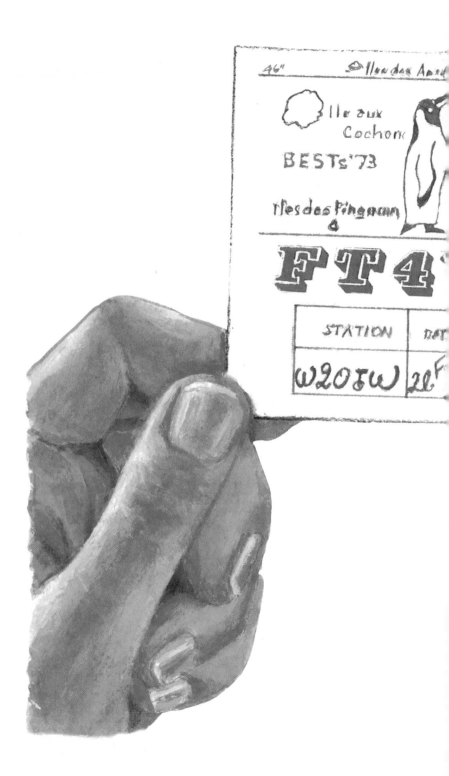

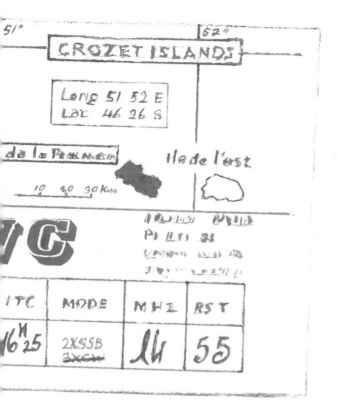

51" | 52"

CROZET ISLANDS

Long 51 52 E
Lat 46 26 S

da la Possession   Ile de l'est

10 20 30 Km

ITC	MODE	MHZ	RST
16 25 H	2XSSB ~~2XCW~~	14	55

This is a QSL card.

Whenever hams connect on the air for the first time, they exchange specially designed postcards in the mail.

These QSL cards are physical proof that the radio contact actually took place.

Each ham's card is different, featuring the call sign for his station, details about the call and the gear used, and words and pictures that tell more about himself and his home.

This is an emergency.

Amateur radios provide a vital backup communication system when phone and power lines are down. Hams relay information to law enforcement and emergency services. This hobby is not only fun, it can save lives.

This is the world.

Say hello.

Published by
Princeton Architectural Press
37 East Seventh Street
New York, New York 10003

For a free catalog of books, call
1.800.722.6657.
Visit our web site at
www.papress.com.

Editor: Jennifer N. Thompson
Design: Office of Paul Sahre

Special thanks to: Nettie Aljian, Ann
Alter, Nicola Bednarek, Janet
Behning, Megan Carey, Penny Chu,
Russell Fernandez, Jan Haux, Clare
Jacobson, Mark Lamster, Nancy
Eklund Later, Linda Lee, Nancy
Levinson, Katharine Myers, Jane
Sheinman, Scott Tennent, and Deb
Wood of Princeton Architectural Press
—Kevin C. Lippert, publisher

Images from *QST Magazine* reproduced with kind permission of the
ARRL (see pages 14, 36, 104, 160).

Illustrations by Arline Simon
(see pages 1–7).

Photograph of the WTC on 9/11/01
by Scott Santoro (see page 16).

Photographs of Jerry Powell appear
courtesy of Donald Powell (see pages
9, 13, 38, 241-248).

Photograph of Guglielmo Marconi
(see page 33) is taken from *L. Solari*,
Marconi, Paul List Verlag Leipzig, 1942.

Photographs of the Market Reef
expedition reproduced with kind
permission of Leif Lindgren (see
pages 217-223).

The photograph of Samuel Morse
is from The National Archives
and Records Administration (see
page 250).

The photograph of Frankfort,
Kansas appears courtesy of Wichita
State University Library.

Photographs of the handheld (see
page 15), vacuum tube (see page
35), hand with mic (see back cover)
and propagation illustrations (see
pages 97-99), by the Office of
Paul Sahre.

All QSL cards, and the radio image
(see page 15), are from the personal
collection of Danny Gregory.

Library of Congress
Cataloging-in-Publication Data

Gregory, Danny, 1960–
  Hello world: a life in ham
radio/Danny Gregory,
Paul Sahre.
    p. cm.
  ISBN 1-56898-281-X
  1. Amateur radio stations. 2.
Radio—Amateurs' manuals. 3.
Radio—Biography. I. Sahre, Paul. II.
Title.
  TK9956 .G6495 2003
  621.3841'6'092—dc21

    2002015361

For Patti Lynn and Jack
DANNY

For my father
PAUL

HELLO WORLD

A LIFE IN HAM RADIO

BY

DANNY GREGORY

AND

PAUL SAHRE

PRINCETON ARCHITECTURAL PRESS

NEW YORK

PREFACE

This book will immerse you in a typical ham experience without having to pass a licensing exam, put thousands of dollars into equipment, or spend 70 years on the air. You will learn about the culture and history of the hobby, and get a sense of what these hundreds of conversations might have been like and how they helped to enrich one man's life.

Hello World is about Jerry Powell's life as a ham radio operator. But because of the nature of amateur radio, it's actually the story of hundreds and, in turn, millions of people all over the world.

There are several intertwining themes to this story: there's the life of Jerry Powell, the hub of this far-flung network; a layman's overview of radio technology; the hobby's rich culture; the QSL cards that confirm each new contact; the individuals who Jerry contacted; and the current events that influenced this global conversation.

The core of the book is a collection of 369 cards, each the size of a standard postcard, that confirm the contact between Jerry Powell and each person with whom he spoke. Together, they are a chronological record of the landmarks in his conversations with the world.

Each QSL—a ham radio term meaning a contact is confirmed— card is unique. It contains specific technical information on the contact, the equipment used, the strength and clarity of the transmission, the identities of the parties involved, etc. But more interestingly, it is also a unique design created for or by the individual operator. Pictures, drawings, and text decorate the cards and tell the person's story.

In less than 24 square inches, these cards convey a lot of information. And we've found there's a story behind every QSL.

Most of the cards include details about the person, their place of origin, and what they were experiencing at the time of the call. Jerry liked to speak to people who lived in places currently in the news, and many of these conversations took place during times of enormous change in the world. We have encapsulated each sliver of history, summarizing front-page news that is now largely forgotten.

Interspersed throughout the collection are essays on aspects of radio technology and ham culture, and glossaries of ham lingo and technology to explicate some of the more obscure aspects of the contacts. The fold-out map that follows page 153 and the alphanumeric guide under each card are cross-referenced to help you pinpoint every contact.

INTRODUCTION

For most of us, ham radio is a mildly intriguing mystery—quaint and probably obsolete. Perhaps, as a kid, you had a nerdy uncle or cousin with a room full of radios or a neighbor with a big antenna in the yard. Maybe you just assume it's part of the whole CB radio craze from the 1970s or another word for those short-wave radios that pull in the African Service of the BBC.

But for most hams like Jerry Powell (FIG. 1), amateur radio is an obsession. As soon as they get hooked, often as boys, hams find themselves with a lifelong pursuit. They build and tweak their gear incessantly. They invest in expensive new transceivers, lining more and more equipment on the shelves of their ham shacks. Their families grow used to hearing distant voices filter through the floorboards from the basement late at night or early in the morning. Many hams carry small, portable units the size of cellular phones; while their wives buy groceries, they wait in the car, talking, tweaking, talking. It's not unheard of for two hams to talk to each other from across a room, preferring the transmitted word to a direct conversation, like boys snickering over their first walkie-talkies.

Jerry's obsession began when he was a teenager and hooked him until his key went silent (a ham euphemism for death) more than 70 years later. He built his daily schedule around distant time zones and cycles of sunspots. While his wife went off on vacation to China and Russia and parts beyond, Jerry stayed in the basement and talked to her destinations on his rig.

One of the key reasons why Jerry was so compelled by ham radio was his on-air community, a vast group of people with a lot in common, and one that's pretty hard to enter. Unlike CB radio or the Internet, amateur radio is only open to those who pass one of the FCC's rigorous licensing tests covering technical knowledge of radio operation, regulations, and other dense areas (each successive test gives one more access to more frequencies).

While the requirements for passing the entry-level test have been relaxed recently to fight off obsolescence, it takes months of study to tackle more advanced questions like: What is the Q of a parallel RLC circuit if the resonant frequency is 14.128 MHz, L is 4.7 microhenrys and R is 18 kilohms?

FIG. 1

Jerry Powell

FIG. 2
QST Magazine,
July, 1965

FIG. 3
QST Magazine,
March, 2002

So when a ham gets on his (and it's rarely *her*) radio, he can be pretty sure what sort of person he'll discover. It won't be some lonely trucker wondering if his good buddy spots any Smokies. And it won't be a conversation cloaked in anonymity or garbled in a crowded chat room, with people whom he'll never encounter again. On the radio, he'll be speaking to others who know a picofarad from a millihenry, but probably more importantly, understand the rules of a community with a century of conventions and a strong sense of responsibility and civic duty. Sociability is a key to ham radio—after all, it's used to chat with complete strangers. But it has a strong sense of protocol and fair play. Many hams get their first radio experience in the Boy Scouts, and that context never fades. There are strict rules about obscenity, indecency, and profanity; about the conventions of how to connect with another; or when it is acceptable to interrupt. You can't even use the airwaves to transact business of any kind. All participants must identify themselves clearly and repeatedly, and their call letters are easily cross-referenced with a database of names and addresses so there is full accountability for every word spoken. All of this self-regulation makes for a community that's friendly and familiar, particularly if you are the sort of person who is quite comfortable spending every evening alone in the basement with the sound and smell of humming vacuum tubes.

For Jerry, part of the fun was undoubtedly the engineering challenge, using his understanding of physics and electronics to coax a new connection out of his setup. He would pore over each new issue of *QST*, the monthly magazine of the American Radio Relay League (ARRL) (FIGS. 2, 3), full of wiring diagrams and photos of antennas. For many hams, their greatest pleasure is to tinker with their equipment, test their work on the air, and then dismantle it and try something else. Their conversations revolve heavily around their gear, peppered with references to circular polarization, frequency synthesis, transverters, and notch filters. They have long debates about multiband Yagis, rotor-mounted quads, inductive attenuators, and the best way to prevent tape slippage in Dymo label makers.

Jerry was an aeronautical engineer and a reasonably hard-core wirehead. He became a ham in a time when there were no thick catalogs full of gleaming digital transceivers ready to be plugged in and

FIG. 4

An early home-
brewed radio
transmitter and
microphone

FIG. 5

A Yaesu VX-5R
handheld
transceiver

fired up. Necessity drove him to become an expert and build much of his equipment himself.

In 1959, Peter Riker was a 13-year-old neighbor. He recalls being terribly impressed by Jerry's homebrew rack-mounted kilowatt station on 20-meter AM, the loud "clack" from the relays on the talk bar on his Asiatic D104, and the purple glow from his mercury rectifier tubes. Jerry gave Peter his test and he is still on the air as K4BKD.

Jerry was more than just a technology geek. At first, his collection of contacts seems random, just a list of the stations he managed to tune in. But a strong pattern lies beneath the surface. Jerry was an avid follower of current events and an in-depth reader of the *New York Times*. He used the newspaper as a guide for his hobby, trying to reach the parts of the world he had read about in the paper. As wars flared up, he tried to get behind the lines, to talk to people who were shut off from the outside, to discuss their experiences, and to offer help.

FIG. 6

A multiband Yagi

Helping where needed is a key component of amateur radio. In fact, public service is the ostensible reason why the Federal Communications Commission (FCC) permits even amateurs to use the airwaves, as a backup communications system in times of emergency. Hams regularly participate in drills to establish a network of communications that can relay messages from third parties. During severe weather, this network saves lives, provides early warning of hurricanes and tornadoes, and links emergency and disaster relief officials.

Hams relay messages from servicemen or ex-patriots in far-off places to their families back home, forming a chain that can get through all sorts of interference. Every time Jerry pulled in a weak and distant station, he was honing skills that could be critical in an emergency.

Ham radio continues to be a thriving hobby, despite the competing communications technologies now available to the general public. There are approximately 675,000 hams in the US today and over 2.5 million worldwide. They continue to play an important role during disasters.

In fact, on September 11, 2001, hams played a vital role in downtown New York City (FIG. 7). Cellular telephone service was down as dozens of police and fire companies began to stream into Manhattan from across the US. Their communications systems were incompatible with each other, and with law enforcement and federal disaster organizations. The Red Cross and Salvation Army enlisted the help of scores of hams, who quickly set up a communications network to span the chaos of that awful day. The hams continued to serve around the clock under hazardous conditions, 20 volunteers to a shift, until a semblance of communications normalcy was returned to the city.

Jerry Powell was not a super ham. He was just an average hobbyist with a long-term commitment, a typical radio amateur who got enormous satisfaction from his pastime. Like many hams, he was a great evangelist for amateur radio, mentoring new hams, sharing news and stories from his on-air adventures with colleagues, neighbors, and friends. This book is a final tribute to that passion, inviting you into Jerry's circle to share his love of radio and of the great friendship it kindled with hundreds of strangers around the world.

FIG. 7

NY-area hams assembled on September 11, 2001

THE QSLs OF WO2JW

AND W9DOG

A CHRONOLOGY

CREATION OF THE FEDERAL
RADIO COMMISSION

This is Jerry Powell's complete collection of QSL cards.

They are reproduced here at either full or half size. Each has the same function and more or less the same dimensions, those of a standard postcard, but it is remarkable how varied they are in design and content.

While the collection is fairly large (369 cards in all), it is probably far from a complete record of all the contacts he made over his 70 years on the air.

Like many hams, he kept only the cards that were special to him, his first contacts with a new country, especially difficult contacts, and QSLs that counted towards a sought-after award. These were his keepsakes, the ones that meant the most to him.

LINDBERGH FLIES ACROSS
ATLANTIC

This is the first QSL card in Jerry's collection, when his call number was W9DOG. It confirms his first QSO (contact), 340 miles from Frankfort to Shawnee. 5GF is an unusually short and early call number, so even as early as 1928 this ham was probably quite seasoned.

001—5GF 6/27/28 (F:156)

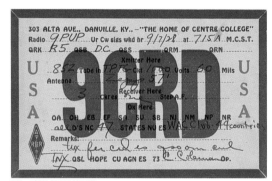

002—9CRD 9/7/28 (C:156)

002—9CRD

This is the card of a fairly hard-core DXer. He has already contacted 47 of the 48 states and 49 different countries. He uses many abbreviations to give Jerry useful information about how his gear is functioning: QRK refers to the intelligibility of the signals, QSB warns if the signals are fading, QRM would indicate interference from other hams on adjacent channels, and QRN signifies static.

9CRD's abbreviations extend to the sign-off: 73 is the code for best regards. He even contracts Jerry's call sign to "9PUP."

FLEMING DISCOVERS
PENICILLIN

FIRST ACADEMY AWARDS

003—1AXR

This card was mutilated by some stamp-collecting Powell; Jerry must have clipped off the penny stamp on the back. Fred E. Davis signs off, "How about a card, Old Man?" —a common term of affection between hams. It seem this Morse-code call across the country was plagued with static.

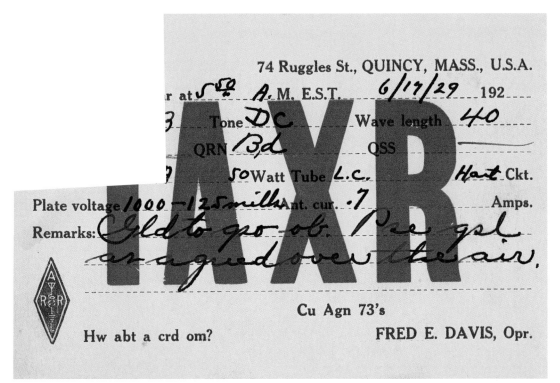

74 Ruggles St., QUINCY, MASS., U.S.A.

r at *5⁰* A. M. E.S.T. *6/17/29* 192

Tone *DC* Wave length *40*

QRN *Bd* QSS —

50 Watt Tube *L.C.* *Hart* Ckt.

Plate voltage *1000—125 mills* Ant. cur. *.7* Amps.

Remarks: *Gld to go ob. I've gsl as argued over the air.*

Cu Agn 73's

Hw abt a crd om? FRED E. DAVIS, Opr.

003—1AXR 6/17/29 (B:156)

ST. VALENTINE'S DAY
GANGLAND MASSACRE IN
CHICAGO

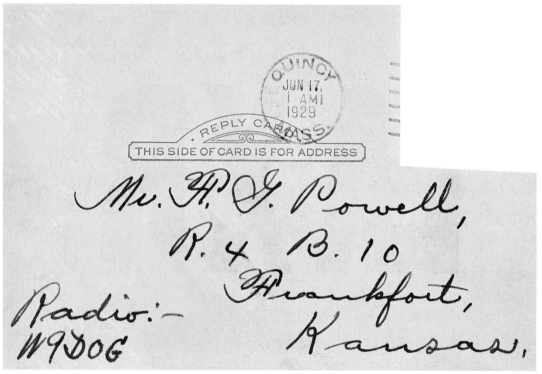

QUINCY
JUN 17,
1 AM
1929

· REPLY CARD ASS·
THIS SIDE OF CARD IS FOR ADDRESS

Mr. H. G. Powell,
R. 4 B. 10
Frankfort,
Kansas,

Radio :-
W9DOG

003—1AXR (BACK)

FIRST CAR RADIO

ADMIRAL BYRD FLIES OVER
SOUTH POLE

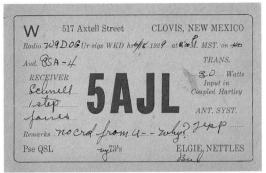

004—5AJL 6/18/29 (B:156)

005—W5BBX 7/17/29 (E:156)

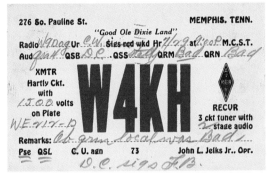

006—W4KH 7/29/29 (C:156)

004—5AJL

Three months after this contact, Elgie Nettles wonders why Jerry hasn't gotten around to sending a QSL card.

005—W5BBX

This call was relayed to Mississippi and seems to have been very friendly. McDougal has embellished his QSL card with a little good luck sticker and tells "Old Top" he hopes to see him again soon.

006—W4KH

Another fairly poor signal from "Good Old Dixie Land."

US STOCK MARKET CRASH, MARKET LOSES $26 BILLION, KICKING OFF THE GREAT DEPRESSION

11/29

007—VK9AB

Jerry becomes a DXer,
pulling in a contact with Alf
Bunting in New Guinea,
8,000 miles from Kansas.

008—VK7JK

This QSL came through the
Tasmanian division of the
Wireless Institute of
Australia. Unfortunately,
it seems not to have been
filled in with any information about the contact or
the sender. Note the photograph of what is probably
Hobart, Tasmania's capital,
augmented with a self-por-
trait of the unknown ham
sitting astride Mount
Wellington.

009—W3HVQ

QRA at the top of the card
means "What is the name
of your station?"—an
appropriate question as
W9DOG was about to van-
ish. Stay tuned.

007—VK9AB 5/30/30 (R:158) SEE 285

008—VK7JK 8/4/31 (R:158)

PLUTO DISCOVERED

Eight and a half years passed between VK7JK and the next QSL in the collection. In the interim, Jerry received a degree in aeronautical engineering from Kansas State where he met and married Mabel; his first son Donald was born the next year. Finding an engineering job in Depression-era Kansas proved fruitless, so Jerry took a position for $750 a year teaching school and coaching basketball in Chanute, Kansas.

It's unclear whether he unplugged his radio during this period or simply pared down his QSL collection when he moved.

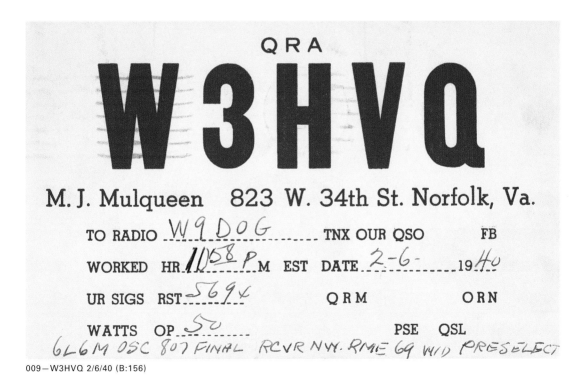

009—W3HVQ 2/6/40 (B:156)

EMPIRE STATE BUILDING
CONSTRUCTED

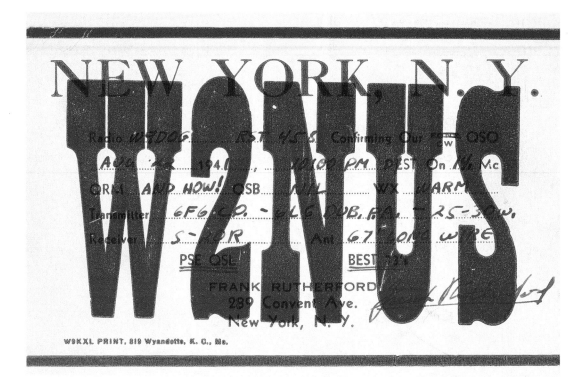

NEW YORK, N. Y.

Radio *W7DOG* RST *4SS* Confirming Our QSO

AUG *22* 194*0*, *10:00 PM* EST On *14* Mc

QRM *AND HOW!* QSB *WILL* WX *WARM*

Transmitter *6F6 CO - 6L6 DUB. P.A. - 25-30 W.*

Receiver *S-20R* Ant *67* *LONG* *WIRE*

PSE QSL   BEST 73

FRANK RUTHERFORD
289 Convent Ave.
New York, N. Y.

W9KXL PRINT, 819 Wyandotte, K. C., Mo.

010—W2NUS

W2NUS lived nearby in uptown Manhattan but their radio contact seemed to have been overwhelmed by interference, so Frank Rutherford invited Jerry to come over and meet the "W2 gang" in person. On the back of the card he drew a map with driving instructions to his home on Manhattan's Upper West Side.

FRANCE SURRENDERS TO
GERMANY

JAPANESE ATTACK PEARL
HARBOR

At the beginning of World War II, Jerry finally secured work as an aeronautical engineer, working as a civilian employee of the US Navy. He was stationed at the facilities of defense contractor Bendix in Teterboro, New Jersey, a job he did through the war and up until his retirement in 1970. He moved his family from Kansas to a new home in Hackensack, New Jersey.

When the war began in Europe in September 1939, the US initially declared its neutrality. Although hams were not restricted, they were encouraged to avoid any discussion of the war over the airwaves.

Meanwhile, although most of European amateur activity was suspended, Nazi hams began to broadcast propaganda. The FCC grew alarmed at the spread of this misinformation and outlawed all contact between US and international amateurs. All hams had to sign a loyalty oath and verify that they were American citizens.

After the attack on Pearl Harbor, all amateur activity was suspended, except for the War Emergency Radio Service. Hams who notified their recruiters or draft boards that they were licensed and experienced were often drafted to assist with communications. Otherwise, they were off the air for the duration of the war.

On August 25, 1945, the ban was lifted, and within a year the military withdrew from most ham frequencies.

A few months after VJ Day, Jerry returned to the air as an official New Jerseyean with his new call number W2OJW.

011—W8ZJK 3/23/46 (E:156)

011—W8ZJK

From Eugene A. Cole
(formerly W9VJD) of
Marquette, Michigan

012—D4ANS

In November 1946, it was
extremely unlikely that any
German nationals would
have been allowed on the
air. However, Don Krueger
was an American staff sergeant who was part of the
Occupation force.

The 3112th Signal Service
Battalion of the US Army
had been constituted in
early 1944 in Fort
Monmouth, just a few miles
from Jerry's home in
Hackensack. Monmouth was
a sort of boot camp for
hams, with a vast ham
shack full of every conceiv-
able piece of equipment and
a forest of antennas.

The 3112th went on to participate in the D-Day attack
on Normandy and provided
communications in cam-
paigns through Northern
France, the Rhineland,
Ardennes-Alsace, and
Central Europe.

After VE day, Don and his
comrades had safer duty at
HQ in Frankfurt. Three
weeks after his contact with
Jerry (which left him wish-
ing he had "more QSOs like
this one"), the 3112th SSB
was deactivated.

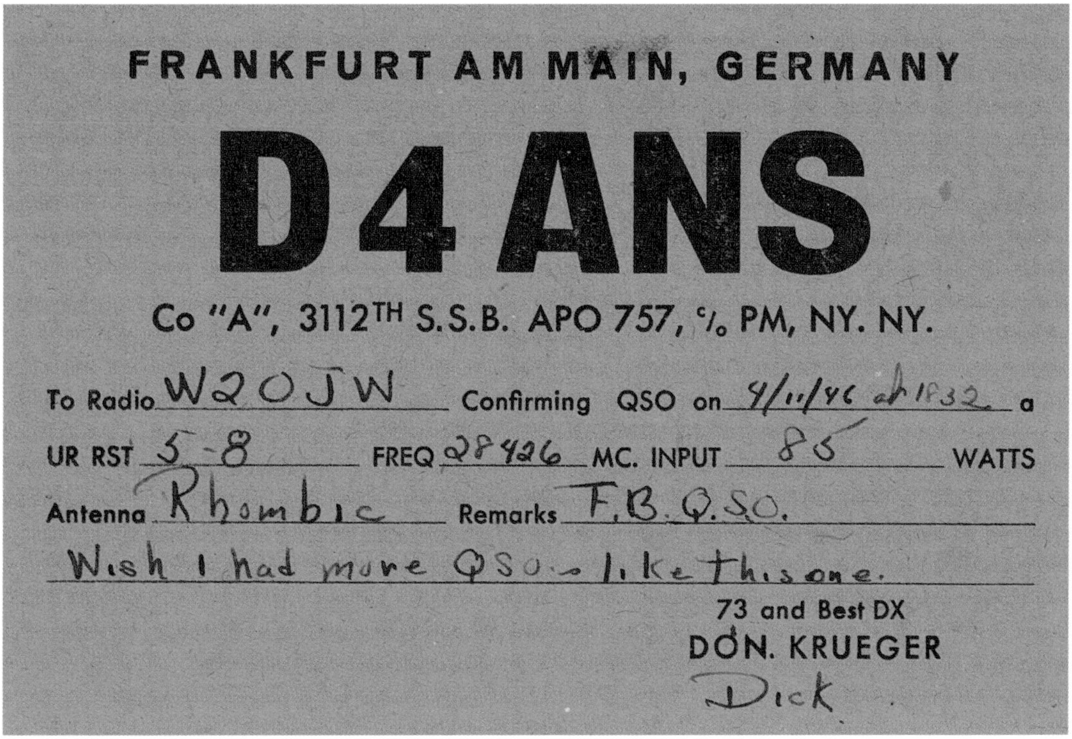

FRANKFURT AM MAIN, GERMANY

D4ANS

Co "A", 3112TH S.S.B. APO 757, ℅ PM, NY. NY.

To Radio W2OJW _____ Confirming QSO on 4/11/46 at 1832 a

UR RST 5-8 _____ FREQ 28426 MC. INPUT 85 _____ WATTS

Antenna Rhombic _____ Remarks F.B.Q.SO.

Wish I had more QSOs like this one. _____

73 and Best DX

DON. KRUEGER

Dick

012—D4ANS 4/11/46 (M:157)

013—W0FQJ

Gene Dodds apologized for the five months it took him to confirm his QSO with Jerry as he had just received these cards from the printer. Postwar America was still a time of great shortages, and printing QSL cards was a low priority, even for hams.

Knoxville, Iowa

W0FQJ

Eugene H. Dodds   1108 Montgomery St.

013—W0FQJ 7/22/46 (F:156)

FINDLAY   *On the Bank of the Old Mill Stream*   OHIO

Radio W2OJW Confirming QSO 8/2 1946 at 10:10 AM E.S.T.
Ur 14 MC. CW FONE sigs R S T Conditions Good

W8VDJ

Xmtr: 6v6 eco - TB35 - TB35 - TB35 - TW150 PP 1 K Mod: 822s class B
Ant: 4 element rotary 80 BQ6/0E 500W DM36 Rcvr: SX28A
TNX FER QSO PSE QSL   ROUTE 6   73 BOB LORA

014—W8VDJ 8/2/46 (C:156)

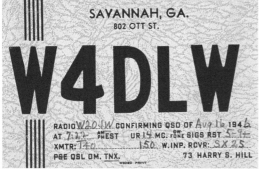

SAVANNAH, GA.
802 OTT ST.

W4DLW

RADIO W2OJW CONFIRMING QSO Aug 16 1946
AT 7:22 PM EST UR 14 MC. CW FONE SIGS RST 5-1
XMTR: 140   150 W. INP. RCVR: SX25
PSE QSL OM. TNX.   73 HARRY S. HILL

017—W4DLW 8/16/46 (D:156)

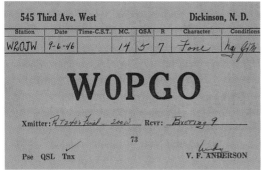

LEASIDE, ONTARIO
144 RANDOLPH ROAD

Radio W2OJW ur Sigs wkd hr Aug 31 1946 at 610 m
QSA 5 R 9 QRM   on PHONE 14 MC Band
Xmtr 150 W
813
3 EL
ROTARY   Rcvr 14 TUBE MEISSNER

VE3AAA

REMARKS TNX FR FB QSO JERRY
PSE QSL TNX   73   W. M. BOOTH

018—VE3AAA 8/31/46 (C:156)

545 Third Ave. West   Dickinson, N. D.

Station	Date	Time-C.S.T.	MC.	QSA	R	Character	Conditions
W2OJW	9-6-46		14	5	7	Fone	hg J/m

W0PGO

Xmtr: RT240 Final 200W   Rcvr: Breting 9
73
Pse QSL Tnx   V. F. ANDERSON

021—W0PGO 9/6/46 (G:156)

KNEESWORTH (CAMBS),
ROYSTON, HERTS. ENGLAND
RADIO W2OJW TNX for QSO 12/9/46 GMT ur RST QS R7
28 Mc

G2CG

Input 100 W ANT 3 EL RMKS
73
Pse QSL Tnx   CHAS. W. HOWES.

022—G2CG 9/12/46 (M:157)

Mr. Curtis was very proud of his hometown.

Founded in 1879 by Henry T. Blythe, a Methodist circuit rider with five wives, Blytheville boomed as cypress and hardwood were felled to rebuild Chicago after the Great Fire. The mill camp rip-

roared with honkytonks and pool halls, but quieted down when all the lumber was gone.

In the twentieth century, farmers flourished in the fertile delta soil and Blytheville became famous for hosting the National Cotton Picking Contest each

year. By the time Jerry contacted David Curtis, the town's fortunes were changing as many of the mills and cotton gins moved or folded. But today Blytheville is home to 22,000 folks and the second largest steelmill in the country.

Bill Booth is still operating out of Ontario today, just as he was in 1946.

015—W5GJL 8/4/46 (E:156)

016—VE4AC 8/13/46 (G:156)

019—W9BGI 8/31/46 (E:156)

020—W6SHW 9/1/46 (I:156)

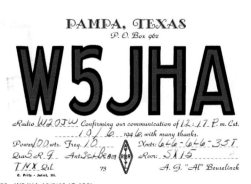

023—W5JHA 10/6/46 (G:156)

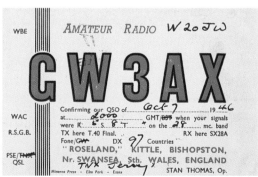

024—GW3AX 10/7/46 (M:157)

This contact with Pete Bonner took place during a hurricane in the fall of 1946. Amateurs are a crucial communication link during times of weather emergency, providing connections to the National Weather Bureau, law enforcement, emergency services, the media, and anxious friends and relatives. Though Bonner's antenna apparently withstood the storm, Key West's phone lines and electricity may well have gone down, so Jerry would have provided a relay for critical information via his own radio and telephone.

"HURRICANE - CONTACT"

QRA *P.O. BOX 415* **U. S. A.** *KEY WEST FLA*

Radio *W2OJW* Ur *P* Sigs *QSA* R *5* S *9* T *9* Band *28 MC*

Date *10 - 7 -* 19*46* At *1526 P.* M. EST. Conds. *HURRICANE*

W4EFH

XMITTER *P.P. 35T⁵ 200 WATTS—*

RCVR *HQ-120-3 ELEM. BEAM*

Additional Wind *JERRY I SURE ENJOYED QSO.*
MY BEAM STOOD THE HURRICANE

PSE TNX QSL VY 73 *LUCK + DX* **J. P. Bonner, Opr.** *PETE*

025—W4EFH 10/7/46 (F:156)

THE EARLY DAYS OF RADIO

Jerry first went on the air near the dawn of the Golden Age of radio, the first time a new technology seized the public imagination and transformed our daily lives. In a time of email and mobile web access, it's hard to appreciate the enormous power that radio had in its early days. For the first time in history, people could access the outside world. For the vast majority, there was no phone service and probably not even electricity. Most of them rarely traveled more than a few dozen miles from their birthplaces over the course of their entire lives. For those fortunate enough to have a telephone, long distance was cumbersome and enormously expensive.

Radio changed everything. Suddenly people were receiving programs and news, hearing recorded music, sermons, and sportscasts, and becoming part of a nationwide popular culture.

Wireless radio had its practical origins in 1896, when Marconi managed to send a signal over two miles (FIG. 8). Three years later he transmitted across the English Channel. That same year, the very first radio do-it-yourself project was published in *American Electrician* magazine, encouraging amateur participation in the emerging technology. Of course, the technology was still very rudimentary, allowing only the transmission of code by pulsing waves of static. Despite Marconi's transmission across the Atlantic in 1901 and the ensuing worldwide interest in radio, it still had little practical application.

FIG. 8
Guglielmo Marconi

By 1908, magazines and clubs emerged to promote amateur participation in radio. Stations appeared across the US with no regulation, and operators assigned themselves their own call letters, transmitting however they chose. Within a couple of years, thousands of stations began to jam the airwaves and, with no system to coordinate them, there was enormous interference as amateurs collided with military and marine transmissions. The Navy began to agitate Congress to regulate the airwaves but the need for order achieved new urgency in 1912 with the sinking of the Titanic (FIG. 9). For the very first time the SOS call went out, and hundreds of lives were saved. But the chaos of transmissions between amateurs, ships, and the competing commercial telegraph companies, and their failure to bring in help from other ships in the immediate area were given partial blame for the enormous loss of life.

FIG. 9
The Titanic

After the tragedy, Congress imposed new restrictions on how the airwaves could be used and drastically limited commercial and amateur operators. Then, during World War I, even stauncher limits were imposed, and the hobby virtually disappeared. All amateurs were ordered to dismantle their equipment, and most hams were in uniform and shipped overseas. But in 1919, grass-roots lobbying of Congress reversed the tide and defeated bills that would have imposed a complete ban on all use of the airwaves except by the navy, a move that would have crushed the development of future communications technology, from television to cellular phones.

The invention of the vacuum tube (FIG. 10) and other break-throughs in engineering gave new momentum to the range and popularity of radio. In 1919, Dr. Frank Conrad, a Westinghouse engineer in Pittsburgh, began to broadcast from his garage and take requests to play music from his record collection. When a local department store advertised those broadcasts, they promptly sold out their inventory of wireless radios. "Amateur Police Radio" emerged as a way to link different law enforcement systems to relay broadcasts of crimes and to identify stolen cars and merchandise. This was also the apex of polar expeditions, and Admiral Byrd and others used amateur radio to stay connected.

Commercial broadcasting hit its stride in 1921 when 300,000 people tuned in to the Dempsey-Carpenter fight. Amateurs helped to relay the broadcast and set up speakers in public places for all to hear Dempsey win in the fourth round. The technology was developing so quickly that new radios were obsolete every six months. Today's PC buyers can sympathize.

With all of these new applications, thousands of stations jammed the airwaves as Washington wrestled with ways to regulate the crowd. The Radio Act of 1927 created the first legal definition of "amateur radio" and established the Federal Radio Commission to reign over the regulation of the airwaves. For the first time, there were also criminal penalties for those who broke the new law.

Today such regulations make a great deal of sense. No one wants to turn on his or her car radio and pick up the ragchewing of anyone with a transmitter. Unregulated airwaves would make it virtually

FIG. 10

The RCA 6CL6
vacuum tube

FIG. 11

The amateur radio
bands

The Ham Radio Bands

Meters	MHz
160	1.8-2.0
80	3.5-4.0
40	7.0-7.3
30	10.10-10.15
20	14.00-14.35
17	18.068-18.168
15	21.00-21.45
12	24.89-24.99
10	28.0-29.7
6	50-54
2	144-148
1.25	222-225
0.70	420-450
0.33	902-928
0.23	1240-1300

impossible for police and fire stations to deal with emergencies and would turn your car radio or your TV set into an unuseable thicket of static. But such regulation was hard to come by. Imagine the controversy of a similar measure intended to regulate today's Internet, to eliminate spam, and make it safe for children and the transaction of commerce.

The modern age of American ham radio dawned in 1927. Amateurs were assigned a good swath of the radio spectrum. But there was still a lot to resolve when it came to the international regulations of radio. While Herbert Hoover (FIG. 12), the Secretary of Commerce (and father of a future president of the ARRL [FIG. 13]), and Congress were strong supporters of the development of the hobby in the US, there was still a lot of conflict abroad. Many governments had no interest in giving their citizens the freedom to speak to whomever they chose around the world with no supervision or censorship. In late 1927, delegates from 74 countries, including President Coolidge, participated in an International Radiotelegraph Conference and hammered out the first international telecommunications law. While it reduced some of the spectrum that US amateurs had just acquired, it still provided enormous new freedoms to users from around the world and provided guarantees and protections the likes of which most hams had never known.

For a teenage boy on a little farm on a rural route outside of a small town in the middle of Kansas, these developments were life changing. Jerry's means were limited. His home wouldn't even have electricity until the late 1930s. But each copy of *Popular Science* and *Popular Mechanics* that arrived in his mailbox was full of articles on how to build his own radio and amplifiers, microphones, and speakers, and ads offered parts so he could assemble his own rig for under 50 dollars. And Jerry was not alone; the country and the world was filled with boys with energy and curiosity who were used to building things with their own hands; boys who were not afraid of technology but relied on it to survive every day on the farm; boys who were in remote places, in tiny communities full of people like them, with humdrum lives and predictable futures. With a little perseverance and ingenuity, Jerry could talk to people in the next county, then the next state, and finally overseas, in places he'd never heard of before. Small wonder this lit a passion in him that never went out.

FIG. 12

Herbert Hoover

FIG. 13

The American Radio
Relay League

W9DOG

Jerry's hometown was Frankfort, Kansas, a small community northeast of Manhattan in the lush valleys of Marshall County (FIG. 14). Its deep prairie grass was crossed by eight historic trails, including the Oregon Trail and the Pony Express Trail. In the 1850s, the tiny town of less than a thousand was founded and named for Frank Schmidt, its real estate agent. Before long, new immigrants began to work the fertile soil and fill the valley with corn, wheat, soybeans, alfalfa, and Hereford cattle.

Frankfort was the quiet home of hardworking farmers, and Jerry started driving a tractor at 11. The biggest excitement in the area came in 1913, when the Chicago White Sox and New York Giants arrived in nearby Blue Rapids on the 1913 World Tour. At Frankfort High, Jerry played football but there often weren't enough kids to field a team.

For a 19-year-old boy interested in the ways of the world, home on Rural Route 4 must have been awfully quiet. Quiet, until 1928, when the squelch of a radio set crackled to life.

Jerry's interest was probably ignited by the swelling popularity of the new technology that was exciting the whole country. He mail-ordered instruction books from the ARRL that prepared him for his licensing exam, and he may well have had a neighbor who helped coach him. He traveled to a nearby city like Topeka or Lincoln to take the test with an accredited volunteer exam coordinator of the ARRL and was then awarded his first call letters: W9DOG.

One of Jerry's contemporaries, "Doc" Cummings VE3XR, had many similar experiences and shared them with us in an essay that Jerry himself might have written.

> When I was around twelve years of age, I remember my grandfather had a crystal radio receiver. He had just bought a more modern tube receiver and rather than junk the old one, he gave it to me to play around with and as he thought, wreck it quickly.
>
> This must have been in the early twenties and he was wrong because I got much pleasure out of the receiver, although the cat's whisker was liable to bounce off the good spot when someone walked heavily across the floor.
>
> After listening to many radio broadcast stations and

38

FIG. 14

Frankfort, Kansas,
early 1900s

FIG. 15

Jerry Powell,
Frankfort, Kansas,
1930s

also some commercial Morse stations with signals that meant nothing to me, I really got interested in radio as a hobby. I bought the 6th edition Handbook and started studying it in earnest, along with all my other school work. Soon I felt I could build a receiver myself, so from a friend who had a friend who was a projectionist in a local movie theatre, I obtained the necessary parts of a one-tube receiver. I had saved the headphones from the crystal set and probably some other parts from it as well. Anyhow, the new set worked, but did it ever hum!

Now I was on my way as a short wave listener to the ham bands and was getting QSL cards from all over the world. One of the very first cards was from W1AD in Vermont. It was dated 2nd July, 1931. In the meantime I had been studying radio theory and getting to learn the Morse code. As far as getting my amateur license was concerned, I was completely on my own. I learned all the theory from the ARRL handbook and, with help from a friend, was able to bring my code speed up to the DOT requirements. I passed the examination on the first try and received my license in 1933 with my call sign being VE3XR.

My life as a radio ham has been a very happy one. I have made countless friends on the air and in person. I feel proud in being able to say that I've been an Uncle Elmer to many beginning amateurs in Ontario.

As I dictate this to my XYL from my wheelchair where I am now confined in my declining years, may I conclude by saying that amateur radio has been a great hobby for me and now, when I am unable to do much else, is a real life line that keeps me happy and helps greatly to pass away the time.

73 to all my old friends.

"Doc" Cummings VE3XR

(Doc is now a Silent Key)

THE AMATEUR'S CODE

The Radio Amateur is:

CONSIDERATE

never knowingly operates in such a way as to lessen the pleasure of others.

LOYAL

offers loyalty, encouragement, and support to other amateurs, local clubs, and the American Radio Relay League, through which Amateur Radio in the United States is represented nationally and internationally.

PROGRESSIVE

with knowledge abreast of science, a well-built and efficient station, and operation above reproach.

FRIENDLY

slow and patient operating when requested; friendly advice and counsel to the beginner; kindly assistance, cooperation, and consideration for the interests of others. These are the hallmarks of the amateur spirit.

BALANCED

radio is an avocation, never interfering with duties owed to family, job, school, or community.

PATRIOTIC

station and skill always ready for service to country and community.

—The original Amateur's Code was written by
Paul M. Segal, W9EEA, in 1928.

SPOKANE WASHINGTON 27MC

QSL No.1004 216 PARK PLACE QSO No.88

W7FGQ

W20JW wrkd 10 Nov 1946 1152 A PST

Rcvr: SX25, DM36   Xmtr: 35 watts.

Try Card?   Rudolph Knaack Rudy

W7AMA PRINT

026—W7FGQ 10/11/46 (I:156)

027—W2MLM

Carl Lindemann was one of Jerry's Hackensack neighbors and radio buddies. Rather than reporting a particular contact, he writes that he is confirming "many times" at "a.m. and p.m. and on multiple bands." He mailed this card to Jerry from Boston, apparently one of a new batch fresh from the printer featuring Carl and his home-brewed equipment.

029—W7JHB

This card from Tucson is extremely unusual, a hand-drawn mimeograph that was then colored in, presumably on each QSL the artist/ham mailed out.

035—ZS1BV

This is the first time that Jerry contacted the African continent and is one of the first real international contacts that he made after the war.

027—W2MLM 10/22/46 (A:156)

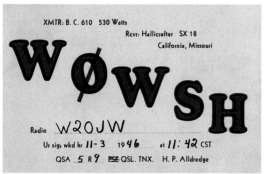

028—W0WSH 11/3/46 (E:156)

029—W7JHB 11/15/46 (H:156)

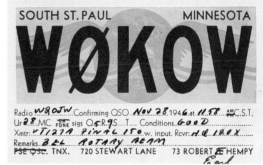

030—W0UQD 11/24/46 (F:156)

031—W0KOW 11/28/46 (F:156)

032—VE7AZ 01/18/47 (I:156)

033—W5BZR 2/2/47 (F:156)

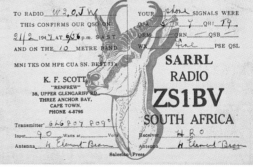

034—VE7RA 2/10/47 (I:156) SEE 032

035—ZS1BV 02/21/47 (O:157)

K6CGK

Now KH6IJ

036—K6CGK 02/23/47 (L:155)

036—K6CGK

Katashi Nose was a major DXer, transmitting with a flawless style from a great DX location on Kauai for six decades. He also had access to an antenna test range that he used to develop a beam-type antenna design that was published in many editions of the ARRL Antenna Handbook.

Nose attended the University of Hawaii, did graduate work at Harvard, and spent much of his adult life as a teacher. He was honored as Radio Amateur of the Year and received the Lifetime Achievement Award at the International DX Convention. He died (or, in ham parlance, his key went silent) in 1994, at age 79.

Despite his death, his call sign is still on the air. As a special honor, it was reissued to his daughter, Frances A. McKenney.

Akaroa, New Zealand is located inside the crater of a volcano extinct for some 6,000,000 years. The Maori have inhabited the area for 1,000 years. Europeans arrived in the late eighteenth century when Captain Cook named the peninsula after the expedition's botanist Joseph Banks. Over the next 30 years a major British whaling colony grew up ultimately leading to a conflict with, and massacre of, the Maori. After a treaty was signed, settlers from England, France, and other countries arrived to create a healthy diversity in Akaroa and built "the Riviera of Canterbury," its narrow streets lined with walnut trees and rose bushes. Today, as in 1947 when Jerry spoke to Syd Langrope, it retains its historical charm and its quiet community of farmers and timber mills.

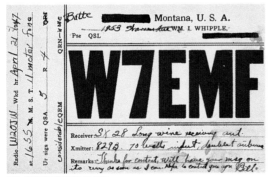

037—W7EMF 04/21/47 (H:156)

038—ZL3IA 04/21/47 (R:158)

PHOTOGRAPH OF RECEIVING HAM

039—VP4TF

Trinidad is home to over 400 species of birds, making it one of the world's richest birding countries per square mile. It's easy to see why the Carib Indians named it "Iere" or "The Land of the Hummingbird."

ADDITIONAL INFORMATION ABOUT CONTACT

PHOTOGRAPHER OR PRINTER CREDIT

RST IS A CODE USED TO INDICATE A STATION'S READABILITY, SIGNAL STRENGTH, AND (IF THE MESSAGE IS IN MORSE CODE) THE TONE OF THE CODE SIGNALS

TRANSMITTER TYPE OF RECEIVING HAM

TYPE OF ANTENNA USED TO RECEIVE SIGNAL. A BEAM ANTENNA IS USUALLY MOUNTED ON A ROTOR AND CONCENTRATES MORE TRANSMITTER OR RECEIVER POWER IN A PARTICULAR DIRECTION

PLEASE

ACKNOWLEDGE RECEIPT (ASKING THE TRANSMITTING HAM TO RECIPROCATE WITH A QSL CARD OF HIS OWN)

CALL SIGN OF TRANSMITTING OPERATOR

STRENGTH OF TRANSMITTER OF RECEIVING HAM

FREQUENCY OR BAND OF CONTACT

THANKS

REGARDS

039—VP4TF 4/25/47 (I:156) SEE 176

CARD NUMBER   CALL SIGN   DATE   "ZONE NUMBER" LOCATION ON MAP   QSL CROSS REFERENCE

OF A QSL

LOCATION OF STATION

CALL OR STATION SIGN OF RECEIVING HAM

MAP OF RECEIVING HAM'S LOCATION

TIME OF CONTACT AT UTC (COORDINATED UNIVERSAL TIME), FORMERLY GMT (GREENWICH MEAN TIME)

A CONTACT BETWEEN TWO OR MORE STATIONS

DATE OF CONTACT

RECEIVER TYPE OF RECEIVING HAM

INDICATES VOICE TRANSMISSION AS OPPOSED TO CONTINUOUS WAVE OR MORSE CODE TRANSMISSION

MC—MEGACYCLES—ARCHAIC TERM FOR MHZ

NAME AND ADDRESS OF RECEIVING HAM

FORMER CALL SIGN OF THE RECEIVING HAM

ADDITIONAL INFO ABOUT RECEIVING HAM: RETIRED FROM THE SIGNAL CORPS OF THE BRITISH ARMY AND NOW A DEALER IN CARIBBEAN ART

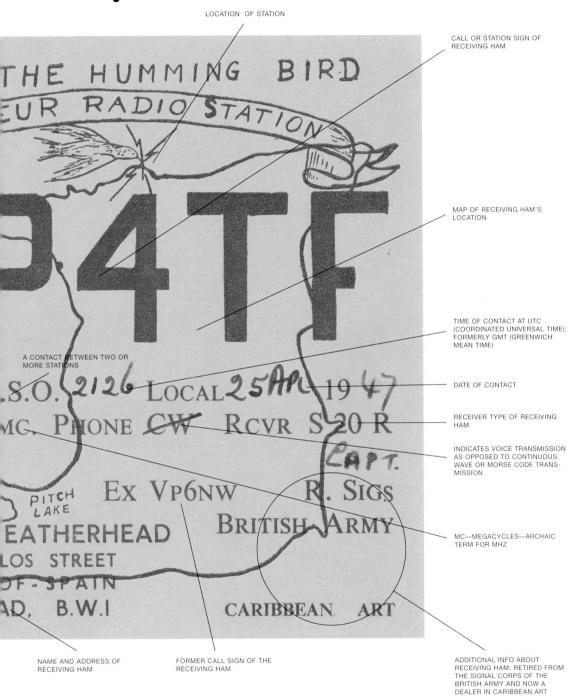

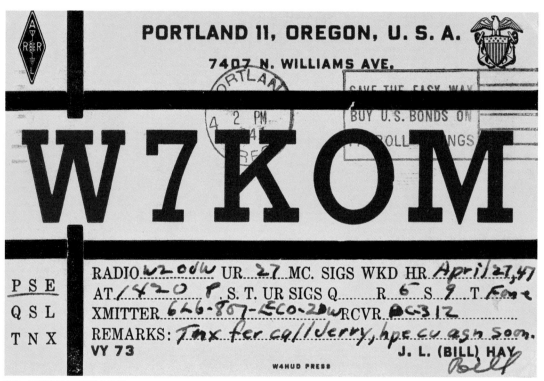

PORTLAND 11, OREGON, U. S. A.

7407 N. WILLIAMS AVE.

SAVE THE EASY WAY
BUY U.S. BONDS ON PAYROLL SAVINGS

W7KOM

PSE
QSL
TNX

RADIO W2ODW UR 27 MC. SIGS WKD HR April 27, 47
AT 1420 P. S. T. UR SIGS Q____ R 6 S 9 T Fone
XMITTER 6L6-807-ECO-2DW RCVR BC-312
REMARKS: Tnx fer call Jerry, hpe cu agn soon.
VY 73   J. L. (BILL) HAY
                                                              Bill

W4HUD PRESS

040—W7KOM 4/27/47 (I:156)

JACKIE ROBINSON JOINS THE
DODGERS, BREAKING THE COLOR
BARRIER

MARSHALL PLAN PROVIDES
AID TO DEVASTATED POSTWAR
EUROPE

4/47   **48**   6/47

This is the first QSL in Jerry's collection from a YL, hamslang for Young Lady (the abbreviation that describes any female operator, regardless of age). Women are definitely the minority in the ham community but apparently things were pretty different in the Phillips home.

041—VE6MP & VE6HZ 8/11/47 (H:156)

INDIA AND PAKISTAN GAIN
INDEPENDENCE

W9MHM

Station Address—R. R. 9, Box 702G, Indianapolis, Ind.

Mailing Address: %  -

3029 EAST WASHINGTON STREET

INDIANAPOLIS, INDIANA

PSE QSL TNX

L. R. GOETZ, OPR.

042—W9MHM 8/18/47 (D:156)

042—W9MHM

While it is forbidden for hams to engage in any sort of commercial enterprise while on the air, some do advertise their business on their QSL cards. In this case, it's quite á propos as Goetz's employer, P.R. Mallory, manufactured tubes for radios.

CHUCK YEAGER BREAKS SOUND BARRIER

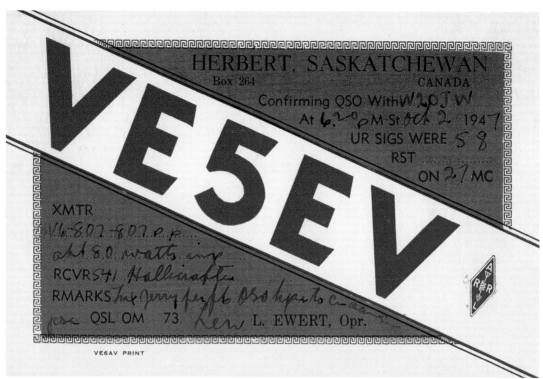

043—VE5EV 10/2/47 (H:156)

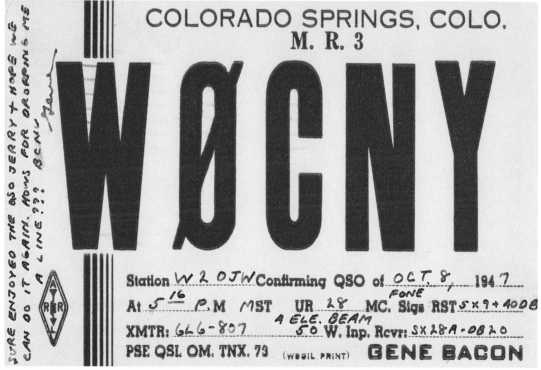

044—W0CNY 10/8/47 (H:156)

WØRQS

STATION	DATE	TIME	R	S	T	BAND
W2OJW	11/2/47	442ϕ	5	9+		Ufone

TRANSMITTER: HT-9 ● **RECEIVER: NC-173**

Cu ogn, Lern. 73 - Frank

F. C. Miller ● Omaha, Nebraska

WAC ● WBE ● WAS   5327 NORTH 52ND STREET

045—W0RQS 11/2/47 (F:156)

38.Pine.Rd.Auburn.Sydney.

VK 2AFE

HULLO

W2OJW
UR fone SIGS-ON 28 mc
1st 12-47 AT 10 AM.
R5 S6 Nice
100% copi hr
Jerry

6SW
8 & 9 PM
3EB

2 ks ud QS20K
hr Jerry. tnx.

5   4
6   5   2
    3
Glad be ud 1st VK   7
on "10" + hpe manimore - 2ks chat + hpe magn - 73 + DX - AUB

046—VK2AFE 12/1/47 (R:158)

BOGOTA - COLOMBIA
SUR AMERICA

HK3IR

TO W2OJW
CONFIRMING 14 MC. QSO
YOUR SIGS. Q 5 R 8
AT 7. P. M. ON Jan/31/48.

QRA. Dr. WILLIAM ELASMAR
CALLE 46 No. 15-66
BOGOTA - COLOMBIA S. A.

TNX QSL PLS.

TIP. FLOREZ, BOGOTA, COLOMBIA

TNX Jerry for F. B. QSO and telephone call. 73's

047—HK3IR 1/31/48 (I:156) SEE 190

046—VK2AFE

This was Jerry's first contact with Australia on the ten-meter HF band. Much of the time, when sunspot activity is low, ten meters is of little use to the DXer, providing direct wave contact of just 25 miles or so. However, when sunspot activity peaks, as it did in late 1947, it provides terrific bounce at the F-layer of the ionosphere, and Jerry was able to reach new distances, luring him away from the 20-meter band, his usual stalking grounds.

047—HK3IR

Bill was the president of the Liga Colombiana de Radioaficionados (LCRA), the Colombian IARU society from 1964 to 1971. For many hams, like Jerry, he was their first contact with Colombia. It's interesting that he also thanks Jerry for a telephone call; it seems less likely that they spoke to each other by telephone than that Jerry called a third party in the states to relay some news from Dr. Elasmar.

GANDHI (A FORMER HAM)
ASSASSINATED BY HINDU FANATIC

048—HL1WH 2/23/48 (Q:156)

048—HL1WH

Colonel Hamlin was part of the US forces that occupied the peninsula south of the 38th parallel. The US had stepped in when 35 years of brutal Japanese rule ended with their surrender in 1945. A few months after Jerry's QSO with Bill Hamlin, the UN supervised the election, which led to the proclamation of the Republic of Korea. But within two years, North Korean communist forces would invade, and Truman would send in US troops.

At the time of Jerry's call with Colonel Hamlin, the seeds of the Korean conflict had yet to sprout. However, it is clear from a series of QSOs over the next couple of years that Jerry was tracking the situation by speaking to military personnel in relevant parts of the world.

050—EL5B

Jerry's second recorded contact with Africa, but he was probably speaking to an American. Roberts Field Airport in Monrovia was built by the US during World War II.

ISRAEL FOUNDED

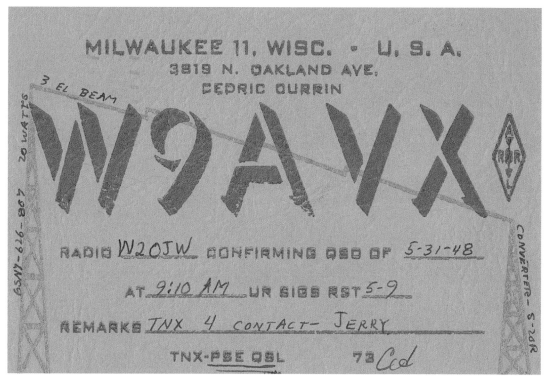

MILWAUKEE 11, WISC. • U. S. A.
3819 N. OAKLAND AVE.
CEDRIC OURRIN

3 EL BEAM

20 WATTS

6SN7-626-807

W9AVX

CONVERTER - S-20R

RADIO W2OJW CONFIRMING QSO OF 5-31-48

AT 9:10 AM UR SIGS RST 5-9

REMARKS TNX 4 CONTACT — JERRY

TNX-PSE QSL   73 Ced

049—W9AVX 5/31/48 (E:156)

ROBERTS FIELD
LIBERIA

RADIO W2OJW CONFIRMING QSO OF 12-7-48

ON 20λ FREQ PH-CW AT 0810 GMT. R 5 S 9 T

EL5B

TNX FOR QSO BEST REGARDS ES LUCK

PSE QSL TNX   JESSE BELL

050—EL5B 7/12/48 (L:157) SEE 089

051—CO7VP 10/20/48 (G:156)

Victor Porter was probably an American busi-
nessman who'd moved to Cuba from the
Midwest. In Jerry's day, relations with Cuba
were radically different from today's. After
the attack on Pearl Harbor, the Cuban government declared war on the Axis powers;
consequently, Cuba became a charter member of the UN in 1945 and in 1948 joined the
Organization of American States. A broad
coalition party was in office but a rocky
world sugar market and spiraling inflation
made for an unstable political situation.

Camaguey was Cuba's third largest city and
an important commercial center and transportation hub. It was one of the original
towns founded by the first Spanish colonists
in the early sixteenth century and much of
the architecture is still preserved. One of its
most unusual features is its confusing, irregular street plan. Supposedly, it was deliberately planned to confuse pirates who might
attack the town.

ZONE TWO

052—VE8MB 10/20/48 (F:156)

052—VE8MB

This card was made with a hand-carved linoleum stamp. The carver, Frank Davis, Jr. may well have had ample time for such craft activities on the frozen shore of Resolute Bay. A popular local T-shirt reads: "Resolute is not the end of the world, but you can see it from here."

In the summer, the vast stretch of gray shale is punctuated by occasional vivid arctic flowers, but in late October 1948, it was becoming an endless sheet of ice and snow.

Davis was probably a member of the weather station at Resolute that was opened at the end of World War II when the Arctic became strategically important for its proximity to the USSR. About this time, an airstrip was built and Resolute established itself as a small community and a gateway for Arctic travelers. In the 1950s, the Polar Continental Shelf Project established a scientific research center and a logistics support base at Resolute Bay. Despite all this activity there was still quite a lot of time and need for the contact that ham radio provided so far away at the top of the world.

Dick was in Southern Greenland to work at the Narsarssuak Air Base nicknamed Bluie West One. It was run jointly by the US and Denmark and, during World War II, sent out planes to escort convoys and take out German U-boats. After the war, it provided a stopover and refueling post for aircraft, and communications for North East Air Command, Air Sea Rescue, and the Air Weather Service.

To fight the tedium of their post, GIs built ski tows from spare Jeep parts and fished for salmon in the glacial lakes with concussion grenades. They also met and mingled with their Eskimo natives and their Danish counterparts.

Some radio operators like Dick had the company of many other colleagues across the North Atlantic, thanks to clear conditions that provided skip propagation all night long. Others had great difficulty with Greenland's magnetic forces and recall being able to talk with planes when they were 50 miles away but not when they were actually touching down on the base runway.

053—OX3MC 10/21/48 (G:156)

In 1896, gold was first discovered at Yellowknife Bay, but because the country was so inaccessible, the gold was left where it lay, all but forgotten. A routine geological survey, 40 years later, found pitchblende on the shores of Great Bear Lake, and prospectors began to arrive in northernmost Canada by the hundreds.

By 1936, Yellowknife was booming, shafts were sunk into the Negus claim, and commercial mining began in earnest. Within a couple of years, the population of Yellowknife had reached 1,000, and the first municipal government in the district was established. But in 1942, progress was stalled as the miners went off to join the war effort and the mines began to close.

By 1948, when Jerry spoke with Bob Lang, the rush was back on, and the town soon outgrew its site. A new town was surveyed and a hydroelectric plant was built to power the new demand. Yellowknife grew into a city and in the 1970s was named the first capital of the Northwest Territories.

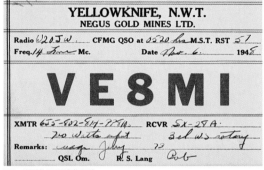

055—VE8MI 11/6/48 (I:156)

058—CX2CO 11/12/48 (M:156)

059—VE2SD 11/12/48 (C:156)

SOUTH AFRICA INTRODUCES
APARTHEID

058—CX2CO

Uruguay was in its golden period at this time with unprecedented prosperity and a purely collegial, Swiss-style executive, which led it to be known as the "Switzerland of South America."

054—VP2KS 10/26/48 (H:156)

056—VP9WW 11/8/48 (E:156)

057—VO6AF 11/11/48 (E:156)

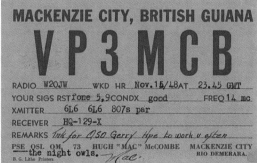

060—VP3MCB 11/15/48 (J:156)

061—VE5GA 12/3/48 (H:156)

062—W3RBE 12/19/48 (C:156)

ALFREDO STAGG C.

P. O.   BOX   340
QUITO — ECUADOR S. A.

HC7KD

THE VOICE OF THE JUNGLE
SHELL MERA — ECUADOR

RADIO <u>W20JW</u> CONFIRMING QSO OF <u>Jan 16th</u> 194.9

AT <u>7.30</u> **AM** **PM** EST UR <u>14</u> MC. **CW** **FONE** SIGS QSA <u>5</u> R <u>7</u>

XMTR; REDIFON - 50 W, RCVR; HRO. ANT. DOUBLET

PSE QSL OM. TNX.   73' S

Alfred

063 — HC7KD 1/16/49 (J:156)

Shell Mera was an oil exploration camp on the edge of the dense rainforests of Ecuador. The Huaorani, a local tribe of Indians, had been extremely isolated for centuries and tended to kill strangers on sight. In the 1940s, they had butchered a number of Shell Oil employees, forcing the company to shut down operations. Around the time of this QSL from HC7KD, the Huaorani, who were even feared by local headhunting tribes, killed several members of another indigenous people, the Quechuas.

Alfredo Stagg was likely one of a group of western missionaries who moved into the area to help the local tribes, treating malaria and snake bites, and setting up schools to teach literacy and sanitation. Shell Mera also functioned as an airstrip for planes that flew short hops to supply other missionaries with mail and medical supplies.

Several years after this contact with Jerry, Shell Mera became infamous. In late 1955, a group of missionaries decided to make overtures of peace to the Huaorani. They flew their small plane over the villages and lowered steel buckets bearing gifts of buttons, photographs, and machetes to the tribes while speaking in local dialect over a battery-powered bullhorn. After three months of aerial contact, the tribes began to reciprocate, placing gifts of parrot feather headdresses into the missionaries' bucket. Encouraged, five missionaries decided to land on a nearby beach. The Huaorani, who associated all outsider contact with killing and cannibalism, panicked at the missionaries' warning shot and speared all five men with wooden lances.

The remaining missionaries were not deterred by this martyrdom. One of the widows stayed in the jungle and wrote three books about the mission work: *Through*

Gates of Splendor, Shadow of the Almighty, and *The Savage My Kinsman.* Dozens of Americans volunteered to take the fallen men's places and, within a month, drops of gifts to the tribe resumed.

The story of the five martyrs of Shell Mera inspired a thousand new volunteers from foreign missions to help build schools and convert the Huaorani, many of whom are Christians today.

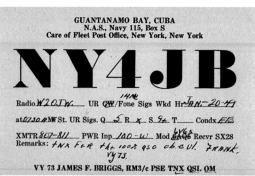

GUANTANAMO BAY, CUBA
N.A.S., Navy 115, Box S
Care of Fleet Post Office, New York, New York

NY4JB

Radio W2OJW UR CW/Fone Sigs Wkd Hr JAN-20-49 14M
at 0730 AM Mtr Sigs Hrd Hr St. Ur Sigs. Q 5 R x S 9 T Condx FB
XMTR 807-811 PWR Inp 100 w Mod 6AQ5 LY65 Recvr SX28
Remarks: tnx for the 100% qso ob.cul. FRANK. VY 73

VY 73 JAMES F. BRIGGS, RM3/c PSE TNX QSL OM

064—NY4JB 1/20/49 (G:156) SEE 182

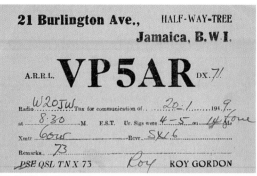

21 Burlington Ave., HALF-WAY-TREE
Jamaica, B.W.I.

A.R.R.L. # VP5AR DX 71

Radio W2OJW Tnx for communication of 20-1 194 9
at 8:30 M. E.S.T. Ur sigs were 4-5 14 fone Ale
Xmtr 6O5C Rcvr SX6
Remarks 73
PSE QSL TNX 73 Roy ROY GORDON

065—VP5AR 1/20/49 (G:156)

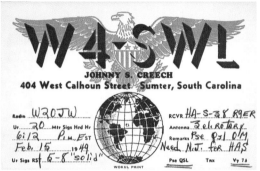

W4-SWL

JOHNNY S. CREECH
404 West Calhoun Street Sumter, South Carolina

Radio W2OJW RCVR HA-S-38 R9ER
Ur 20 Antenna 3 el. Rotary
6:12 P.I.M. EST Remarks Pse Q.71 O/M
Feb. 15 1949 Need N.J. for HAS
Ur Sigs RST 5-8 "solid" Pse QSL Tnx Vy 73
WORXL PRINT

067—W4SWL 2/15/49 (D:156)

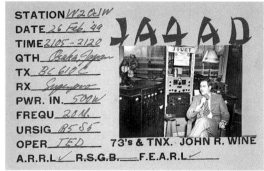

STATION W2OJW
DATE 26 Feb. '49 JA4AD
TIME 2105 - 2120
QTH Osaka Japan
TX BC 610 C
RX Supepro
PWR. IN. 500W
FREQU 20M.
URSIG R5 S5
OPER JED 73's & TNX. JOHN R. WINE
A.R.R.L. ✓ R.S.G.B. F.E.A.R.L ✓

068—JA4AD 02/26/49 (Q:158)

Alfonso Retamal
CASILLA 216
VALPARAISO
República de CHILE

CE2BQ

RADIO W2OJW
Confirmo nuestro QSO en telefonía del March 15th. '49 8.
a las 20.20 en la banda de 14 MC FONE
Sus señales qsa-5; S-7/8 qrm
Receptor Hallicrafters Sx-28
Transmisor 600 Watts
Antena Rotary Beam-3 elements Muy atentos saludos
73s opr.

070—CE2BQ 3/15/49 (L:156)

MARSHALL ISLANDS
KX6AF
KWAJALEIN ATOLL

Radio W2OJW Confirming QSO 7/4 GMT 0018 194 9
UR Q R5 S 8 T 20 Fone CW 10 Fone CW.
PSE QSL TNX QSO 73 W7NMJ
OPR Jim White M / SGT. W. C. GUSTAFSON
AACS NAVY 824, S.F. CALIF.

071—KX6AF 4/4/49 (R:158) SEE 139, 155, 156

FIJI ISLANDS
W2OJW
SUVA :: FIJI
VR2BJ

Confirming two-way Phone communication.
Date 4/7/49 Frequency 14 mc. Time 2325 RST 5.8/9.
Remarks Glad to be first Fiji qso F. M. GRAY,
gary. 73 nolsen. P.O. Box 118.

073—VR2BJ 4/7/49 (R:158) SEE 169

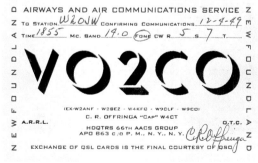

AIRWAYS AND AIR COMMUNICATIONS SERVICE
To Station W2OJW Confirming Communications 12-4-49
Time 1855 Mc. Band 19.0 Fone CW R 5 S 7 T

VO2CO

(EX-W2ANF - W2BEZ - W4KFO - W9CLF - W9COI)
A.R.R.L. O.T.C.
HDQTRS 66TH AACS GROUP
APO 863 C/O P. M., N. Y., N. Y. C. R. Offringa "Cap" W4CT
EXCHANGE OF QSL CARDS IS THE FINAL COURTESY OF QSO

074—VO2CO 4/12/49 (E:156)

066—ZD1SW 1/22/49 (L:157) SEE 112

069—DU1HR 3/13/49 (Q:158)

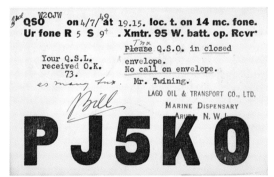

072—PJ5KO 4/7/49 (H:156)

075—PY2CK 4/20/49 (L:156)

FIRST NONSTOP FLIGHT AROUND
THE WORLD

WAC – WAS – WAZ FONE _35_ CW _35_ – COUNTRIES –FONE_101_ CW _102_

075—PY2CK (BACK)

067—W4SWL

On the back of this card, Johnny Creech urgently asks Jerry to be sure to send him a QSL card as he desperately needs to prove a contact with someone in New Jersey. He explains that he is going for "HAS," which probably refers to what is now known as the WAS or Worked All States award.

This is one of several awards given out by governing bodies like the AARL or publications like *CQ* and much coveted by hams. Johnny would have had to submit 48 QSLs to authenticate his log and prove that he had, in fact, made enough contacts to cover the whole country. The most basic award means proving contact on any band or mode for each of the states. The next level is to work each state on a particular HF band from 160 down to 10 meters.

WAC is short for Worked All Continents (not including Antarctica) and is fairly basic for a good DXer. There are 40 CQ zones of the world and the WAZ award goes to anyone proving that he worked all of them. WPX awards go to those who have worked at least 300 different prefixes (W2, W4, etc.). Once a ham achieves 600 prefixes, he is eligible for the WPX Honor Roll. DXCC or the DX Century award is awarded for working at least a hundred different countries, and again contact can be made across all bands.

068—JA4AD

This is Jerry's first contact with Occupied Japan. John Wine appears to have been a civilian who formerly operated out of Granada. He was a member of the American, British, and Far East Asian radio associations. This QSL is also unusual as the photo is hand-pasted onto the card and Wine mentions that the call lasted a full 15 minutes, no doubt filling Jerry in on the extraordinary life of an American living in war-torn Osaka.

069—DU1HR

Jerry made this contact on his 40th birthday.

071—KX6AF

There seem to have been a lot of enthusiastic hams at the US Army base in Kwajalein Atoll in the Marshall Islands of the South Pacific, and Jerry had many contacts with them over the next decade. Kwaj became the western end of the Pacific Missile Range and home to the Nike Zeus/Nike-X, Sentinel, and ABM. In 1956, Jerry would contact KX6BU, the call of the navy's "ham shack," a 12-by-12-foot block house located in the coconut grove on the ocean side of the atoll.

Incidentally, this card took quite a while to arrrive— Jim White filled in a QSL card requisitioned from Sergeant Gustafson, then didn't get around to mailing it until the following year when he returned to his home in Butte, Montana.

073—VR2BJ

Jerry's first contact with Fiji, one of two he would make with Malcolm Gray in Suva (see also 169).

076—HC1KW

It was his wife's 39th birthday, but at 6:45 A.M. Jerry snuck into his shack to speak to Major Rachford in Ecuador. When he was finished he, no doubt, made Mabel breakfast in bed.

078—MF2AA

In 1945, Yugoslav troops captured and claimed Trieste. While the city itself is primarily Italian culturally, the surrounding area is predominantly Slovenian. However, the Allies disagreed with Yugoslavia's claim, and in 1947 the UN carved the new Free Territory of Trieste into two zones, one Italian speaking and overseen by the British and the US, while Yugoslav troops controlled the other. Bob Carragher was a British member of the UN peacekeeping forces who had previously operated out of Italy and Mexico. In 1954, Zone A was folded into Italy and Zone B into Yugoslavia and the Free Territory vanished as a separate DX designation.

079—VE1ME

This card from "the Shack on the Hill" was a great accomplishment for Jerry, the culmination of a goal he set for himself in 1946.

In just over two years, he'd managed to get his WAVE certificate, acknowledgment that he had contacted someone in every single Canadian province (or Worked Every VE). From

VE4AC in Manitoba, VE3AAA in Ontario, VE7AZ in British Columbia, then VE5EV in Saskatchewan, VE6MP in Alberta, E8MB in the frozen Northwest Territories, VE2SD in Quebec, and finally VE1ME in Nova Scotia. This is the only certificate that Jerry seems to have gone after so deliberately.

081—VK6DX

Kalgoorlie was first known as Hannan's Find, when Irish prospector Patrick Hannan and a couple of his mates discovered gold in 1893. When word got out, the biggest gold rush in western Australian history began.

For the next decade, the population of Kalgoorlie grew alarmingly as tens of thousands arrived from around the world. The enormous revolving drums of the stamping machinery beat a constant din and threw smoke and more red dust into the air. The open desert beyond was daunting, a wasteland broken only by patches of stunted mulga and salmon gum trees. The town grew quickly; to this day Kalgoorlie remains synonymous with gold, pubs, brothels, and scorching heat. The nineteenth-century buildings have been restored, the mines still operate, and the town's fortunes still ride the price of precious metals.

QUITO - ECUADOR   SOUTH AMERICA

H C 1 K W

RADIO _W 2 O J W_   UR FONE Q _5_   s _9+_

_14_ MC FONE   AT _0645_ E.S.T.

ON _29 april_ 1949.

XMTR _600 w   BC -610_   RCVR _Super Pro - Doublet ant_

PSE QSL _Jerry_   _73_ _al_   MAJ. AL ROCHFORD, C.E.
                              C/O IAGS, U.S. EMBASSY.

Editorial Carval-Quito.

076—HC1KW 4/29/49 (J:156)

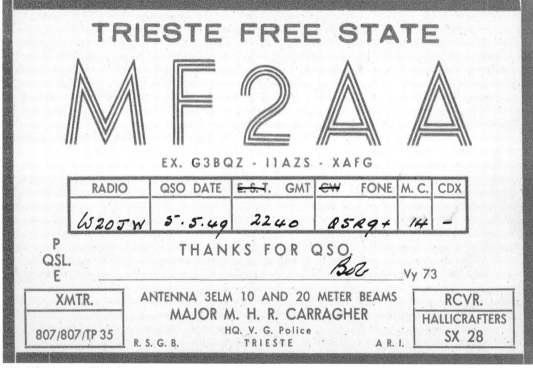

TRIESTE FREE STATE

MF2AA

EX. G3BQZ - I1AZS - XAFG

RADIO	QSO DATE	~~E.S.T.~~ GMT	~~CW~~ FONE	M.C.	CDX
W2OJW	5.5.49	2240	Q5R9+	14	-

P
QSL.
E

THANKS FOR QSO.

Bob   Vy 73

XMTR.	ANTENNA 3ELM 10 AND 20 METER BEAMS	RCVR.
807/807/TP 35	MAJOR M. H. R. CARRAGHER HQ. V. G. Police R.S.G.B. TRIESTE A R I.	HALLICRAFTERS SX 28

078—MF2AA 5/5/49 (N:157)

DAKAR (Sénégal)
FRENCH WEST AFRICA

FF8FP

RADIO _____ CONFIRMING OUR FONE/CW QSO ON _____

AT _____ G.M.T. _____ 1948 UR SIGS RST _____ POWER 50 WATTS

PSE TNX QSL C/O _____ 73s _____

B.M. 583

DAKAR (SÉNÉGAL)

PANAIR DO BRASIL — BANDEIRANTE (CONSTELLATION)

077—FF8FP 5/5/49 (L:157)

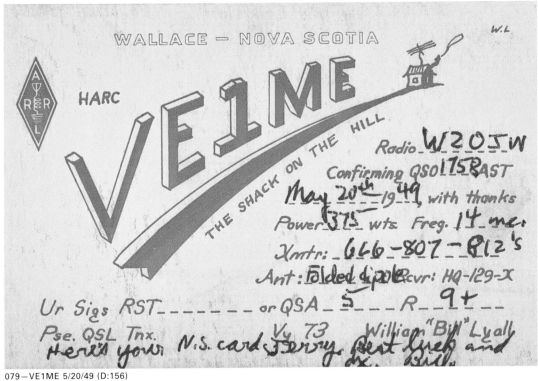

WALLACE — NOVA SCOTIA   W. L.

HARC

VE1ME

A R R L

THE SHACK ON THE HILL

Radio W2OJW

Confirming QSO 175B AST

May 20th 19 49 with thanks

Power 375 wts Freg. 14 mc.

Xmtr: 646-807-812's

Ant: Folded dipole Rcvr: HQ-129-X

Ur Sigs RST _ _ _ _ _ _ _ or QSA _ 5 _ _ R _ 9+ _ _

Pse. QSL Tnx.   Vy 73   William "Bill" Lyall

Here's your N.S. card Jerry, Best luck and dx. Bill

079—VE1ME 5/20/49 (D:156)

MEXICO

Radio W 2 O J V
Q. S. A. 5-4. R

Fecha 5-21-49
Hora 4.40 A.M.

XE1DE

Transmisor RADIOTECNICA, S.A.

Potencia 1000 Watios de entrada

Comentarios

CIPRES No. 164
MEXICO, D. F.

73—Y BUENA SUERTE
DONALD M. STONER

080 — XE1DE 5/21/49 (H:156)

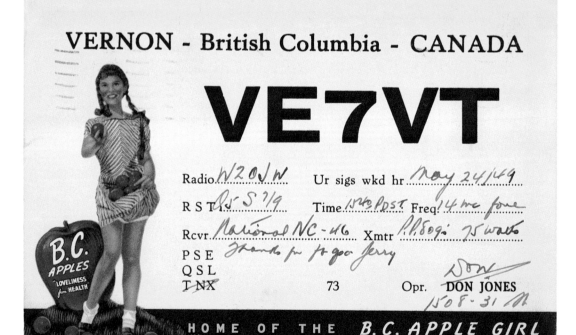

VERNON - British Columbia - CANADA

VE7VT

Radio W2OJW   Ur sigs wkd hr May 24/49
R S T R5 S 7/9   Time 1543 PDST Freq 14 mc fone
Rcvr National NC-46   Xmtr P.P.809. 75 watts
PSE thanks for ft goo Jerry
QSL
TNX   73   Opr. DON JONES
                                1508-31 M

HOME OF THE B.C. APPLE GIRL

082 — VE7VT 5/24/49 (I:156)

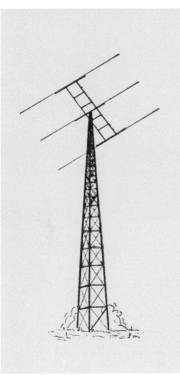

W. H. BARBER,
15 Whitlock Street, Kalgoorlie,
Western Australia.

VK6DX

1922   VK5WH   1937
Greetings from Australia
Regards......*Bred*

081—VK6DX 5/22/49 (R:158)

LU6AJ

Santa Fe 1573, Piso 1°   Buenos Aires

Radio........*W2OJW*
Confirming with pleasure our QSO *FONE*
on *27·Ⅴ·49* at lu-time *20⁻ RM.*
Your signals were RST *58*
Xmtr- 1000 Watts input. Freq. *14 mg,*
Rcvr. *75A1*
                    Enrique A. Correa Keen

083—LU6AJ 5/27/49 (M:156)

MARTINIQUE

F9QU-FM8

Radio W2 OSW Confirming Phone | CW QSO of 1 - VI 19 49

Time 19 25 Your 2 meter MC Signals were RST 5 - S9

Watts input 100 w Antenna half wave doublet PSE QSL-VY 73

Transmitter home made Receiver SX25

2 11 in P. A. TKS for your QSL

084—F9QU-FM8 6/1/49 (H:156)

HAMS

247—ZP5RG

171—K4TLN

234—GL4NRB

295—AH3C/KH5J

041—VE6MP

258—OH0NJ

099—ZS5U

208—OH1MA/CT3

068—JA4AD

131—W0VQC

121—W0OUD

039—VP4TP

027—W2MLM

075—PY2CK

247—ZP5RG

358—S21ZG

283—XF4L

118—W1MIQ

315—9N1MM

In 1937, Iris Hayes of East London became the first YL to be licensed in South Africa. Until she died in June 1999, she was still arranging flowers, making ceramics, driving her car, and being active on the HF and VHF bands. At 95, Iris was the world's oldest living female radio amateur.

In this call in 1949, it seems that Jerry relayed a message from Iris to her friend Lynore, recently transplanted to the US from South Africa, and greatly cheered her up with news from home. Being a bridge for people on distant shores is a typical ham courtesy and seems to have led to many close relationships for Jerry over the years.

S.A.R.L.

First Y.L. in S.A. 1937.

ZS2AA

IRIS HAYES   POPLAR GROVE   WHITTLESEA
C.P.

TO *W.2.0.J.W.*

Confirming QSO on *2.6. w. Mc* B, at *2pm SAT.*

on *25/6/49*. UR Sigs RST *5-8*   Cond. *413.*

XMTR *6L6·807.* *45 Watt input*

RX *N.C.46*

ANT *R. Zamluč.*

Thx Jerry for Swell QSO & all you did for Lynare & we. 733 Irio.

W.A.C.

QP&PCO.

085—ZS2AA 6/25/49 (O:157)

11/7/49.

Dear Jerry.
You certainly cheered Lynore up.
She wrote to say how thrilled she was
when you phoned her & greatly appreciated
your kindness. She loves the U.S.A &
things everything marvellous. I had an
R9 QSO with her from W.6.P.O.B in
Eagle Rock. She stayed with Ken.

Tnx agn om. 73's Iris.

085—ZS2AA (BACK)

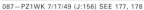

087—PZ1WK 7/17/49 (J:156) SEE 177, 178

088—CX2AF 7/18/49 (M:156) SEE 058

086—KH6NP

Servicemen at Schofield
Barracks were the first vic-
tims of the early morning
raid of December 7, 1941.
On their way to attack Pearl
Harbor, Japanese pilots
flew over Oahu and
bombed the base. Look for
Schofield's quadrangle in
the 1951 movie "From
Here to Eternity."

088—CX2AF

This oversized illustrated
card is quite unusual,
measuring $4^{1}/_{4}$ by $6^{1}/_{2}$
inches. Only two other QSL
cards in the collection are
larger than the standard
dimensions for international postcards (under $3^{1}/_{2}$ by
$5^{1}/_{2}$ inches).

089—EL5A

Remember this—you've played me for a patsy and it cost three lives. Now I'm backing up the hearse for you, and I want it still warm when I dig your grave.—Cobra Venom

This must have been an interesting QSO, for John B. West was many things. He was an amateur radio operator. He was also a colonel, a doctor, and a specialist in tropical diseases. And he was a black man who lived in Liberia.

West was the owner of a broadcasting company, a manufacturing firm, a hotel, and a restaurant. He was also an amateur boxer and a big-game hunter.

And, finally, John West was the author of *The Deadly Sex, Bullets Are My Business, Death on the Rocks, Never Kill a Cop, An Eye for an Eye,* and *A Taste for Blood*, all gritty novels in a long series about a hardboiled white private eye, one Rocky Steele of New York.

090—KG6FA

Despite the incomplete date, the design of the card suggests that this QSO was made in 1949.

091—VE8MC

This photostat card is from Prince Patrick Island, a 7,000-square-mile island in the Arctic Ocean, west of Melville Island in the Northwest Territories. It was discovered in 1853 and named for Queen Victoria's third son. Bob worked in the US Weather station, basically alone on the tundra but for musk ox, Peary caribou, and a few species of geese.

097—KR6CE

Charlie Raymond was a Philco radio field engineer stationed on Okinawa.

089—EL5A 8/16/49 (L:157) SEE 050, 130, 141, 151

090—KG6FA 9/11/49 (R:158) SEE 107

091—VE8MC 9/12/49 (J:156) SEE 130

092—ZS2F 9/14/49 (O:157)

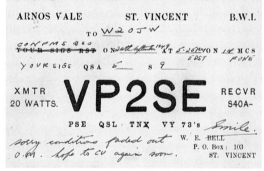

093—W5FYV:VR4 9/16/49 (R:158)

094—HI6EC 9/24/49 (G:156)

095—VP2SE 9/24/49 (I:156)

096—HP1LL 10/22/49 (H:156) SEE 103

097—KR6CE 10/22/49 (Q:158) SEE 125, 145, 273

CN8EA was the first of several contacts that Jerry made in the late 1940s with American servicemen in Morocco. The battlefield for the Allies' first offensive operation against Germany, Morocco remained a crucial strategic post for the US during the Cold War.

In November 1943, the Allies successfully staged Operation Torch, the largest amphibious operation ever undertaken. In extremely short order, 35,000 US troops seized Morocco and turned it into an Allied supply base and a rendezvous point for heads of state. Torch was a turning point that kept Hitler on the defensive for the rest of the war.

In 1949, when Jerry was in contact with Jerry Randle, Gilbert Collier, Bill Smith, and others in Morocco, the Korean War was heating up. Unbeknownst to most Americans, Morocco had become the very first country where the US had been storing nuclear weapons since 1945.

Port Lyautey, located within close proximity to Europe and the Middle East, was an important communications base, and these radio experts were playing a vital role as the ears of Washington.

Port Lyautey was returned to Moroccan control in 1965, renamed Kenitra, and became a base and training school for the Royal Moroccan Air Force.

CN8EA

Port Lyautey, French Morocco
"JERRY" RANDLE
Navy 214, F.P.O., New York, N. Y.

098—CN8EA 10/25/49 (L:157)

PEOPLE'S REPUBLIC OF CHINA
PROCLAIMED

SOVIETS ESTABLISH GERMAN
DEMOCRATIC REPUBLIC IN EAST
GERMANY

10/49

86

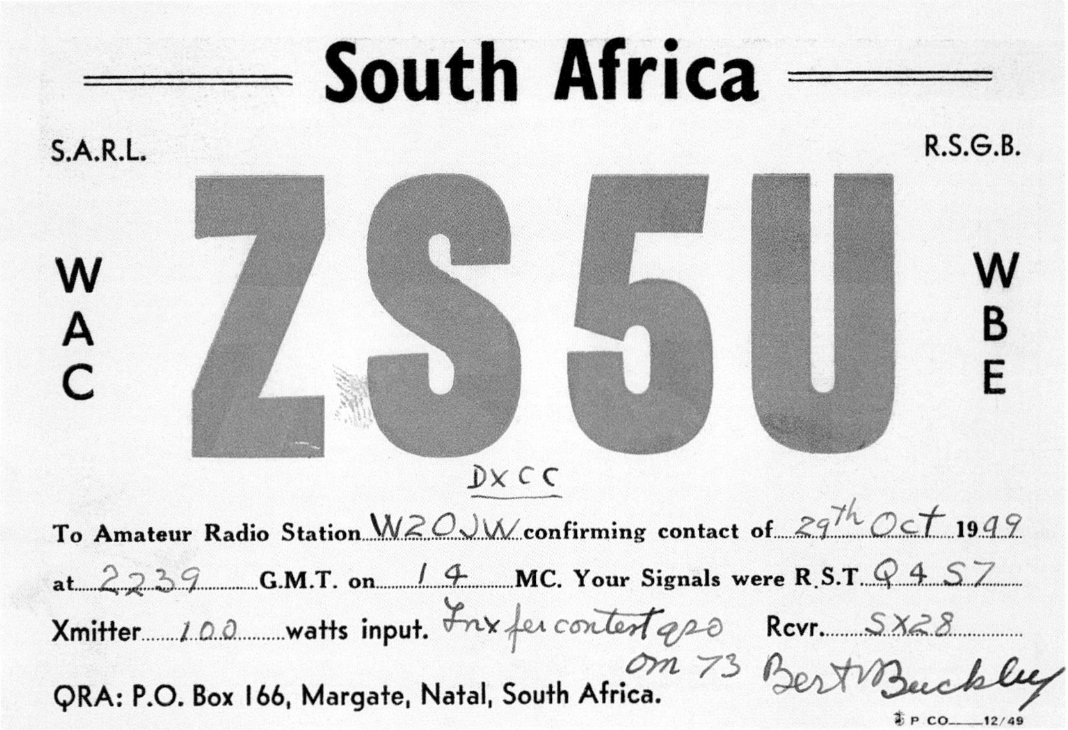

South Africa

S.A.R.L. R.S.G.B.

W A C ZS5U W B E

DXCC

To Amateur Radio Station W2OJW confirming contact of 29th Oct 1949

at 2239 G.M.T. on 14 MC. Your Signals were R.S.T Q4 S7

Xmitter 100 watts input. Tnx fer contest qso Rcvr. SX28

om 73 Bert Buckley

QRA: P.O. Box 166, Margate, Natal, South Africa.

P CO——12/49

099—ZS5U 10/29/49 (O:157) SEE 197

W 2OJW

099—ZS5U (BACK)

S.A.R.L.
QSL BUREAU
P.O. BOX 3037
CAPE TOWN, S.A.

The photo on the back of this card shows Bert Buckley with his contesting trophies. Contests are held to promote certain kinds of communication, encouraging contestants to contact as many hams as possible on a certain band or mode within a specific time, usually 24 to 48 hours. The contacts are as brief as possible to secure a verifiable connection, swapping signal and gear reports, output power, and station codes. There is no time for any sort of social conversation before the next contact must be made.

Thousands of hams from around the world will cram into a band to try to score as many points as possible. There are many types of classes within contests. Some contestants (see 197—UK5MAF) work together as a group in special multi-operator divisions. Competitors using very low power stations have their own competitions as do mobile contestants, operating on equipment with batteries, generators, and other alternate energy sources.

Contests are open to all, and rules and schedules are published in all of the ham magazines. While it's loads of fun, the real function of these competitions is to encourage hams to break their habits, to be prepared to operate under difficult conditions, to handle enormous traffic, and to expand the hobby in new ways that will ultimately provide for emergency communications in a crisis. If there was ever a dam break or an earthquake in Natal, Bert Buckley would be a great guy to have around.

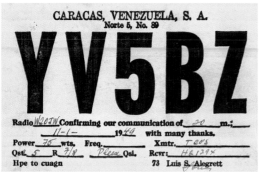

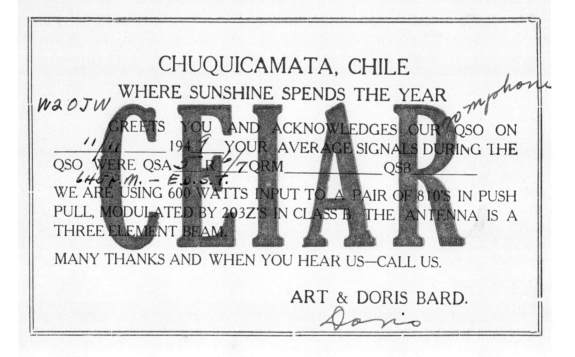

My father was the power superintendent of a very isolated mining camp in northern Chile and communication was not easy. We didn't have stores to go to buy an already-built radio, so Dad built them himself and for other people in the camp.

The radio room was a favorite place for all of us. We spent night after night talking to people from the US, across Europe and the Mideast and on vacation we would visit them. All the ham operators had cards with their call letters and info about their whereabouts. Dad would get these cards in the mail and put them up on the wall in his radio room.

Sometimes someone in the camp would receive a telegram that a family member in the States was sick and would ask my dad if he could learn the status of the patient. Dad would get on the radio and send out a call for someone in that area of the States. Hams are generous people; even if the person receiving Dad's call did not live in that specific town, he would call long distance to learn of the patient's status. If the patient's illness was lengthy, these ham radio Samaritans would call Dad every night on schedule to let the family in Chile know how the patient was doing.

When Admiral Byrd was on expedition in Antarctica and having trouble contacting the States because of atmospheric conditions, he contacted Mother by chance and she had a regular contact with his radio operator, Elmer. Then in the evenings she would reach their headquarters in the States and pass on the news.

I haven't used a ham radio since we were kids and I guess most ham operators have gone the way of buggy whips since now everyone uses email. Still, just thinking about our old radio rooms brings back fond memories of life with Mom and Dad in Chuqui.

—Jeanne Bard Whitsett, daughter of CE1AR

TRANSISTORS BEGIN TO
COMPETE WITH RADIO TUBES

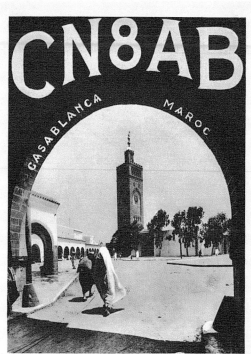

TO RADIO _W2 OJW_ Confirming _14 mc._
Our QSO of _Nov. 12_ 19_48_ at _21ʰ15 gmt_
UR FONE C̶W̶ Sigs.. Q.S.A _5_ S _9x_ R S T
QRA: 53 rue de l'Estérel OPR: J. HERRERA
RMKS: _Tnx fer nice QSO._   _Joe_

102—CN8AB 11/12/49 (L:157)

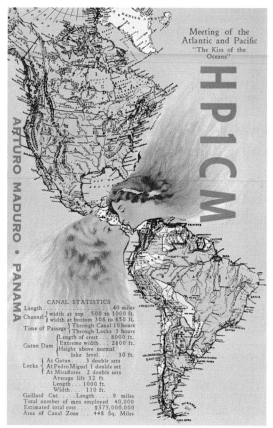

Meeting of the
Atlantic and Pacific
"The Kiss of the
Oceans"

CANAL STATISTICS

Length . . . . 40 miles
Channel { width at top . . 500 to 1000 ft.
{ width at bottom 306 to 650 ft.
Time of Passage { Through Canal 10 hours
{ Through Locks 3 hours
Gatun Dam { Length of crest . . . 8000 ft.
{ Extreme width . . . 2600 ft.
{ Height above normal
lake level . . . 30 ft.
Locks { At Gatun . . . 3 double sets
{ At Pedro Miguel 1 double set
{ At Miraflores 2 double sets
Average lift 32 ft.
Length . . . 1000 ft.
Width . . . 110 ft.
Gaillard Cut . . . . Length . . . . . 9 miles
Total number of men employed 40,000
Estimated total cost $375,000,000
Area of Canal Zone . . . 448 Sq. Miles

103—HP1CM 11/25/49 (H:156) SEE 096

102—CN8AB

After Joe Herrera, the call sign CN8AB belonged to Prince Moulay Abdellah of Morocco, one of the many Middle Eastern royals who caught ham fever from King Hussein of Jordan. The King even operated as JY1 in his final days at the Mayo Clinic. His Majesty King Hassan II of Morocco was CN8MH.

104—KL7ZM

On December 17, 1949, when Hal Burt spoke with Jerry from Fairbanks, Alaska, the state was far from being a bona fide part of the US. Big mining and fishing corporations plundered the natural resources with little oversight and did nothing in terms of social or economic investment. There were no adequate roads or hospitals and proper trade was impossible without airfields or dependable and affordable shipping. The territory had been hard hit by the Depression and many unemployed Americans had been transplanted there by the government in hope of giving them a fresh start at self-sustained agriculture. But beyond a few WPA programs, development was limited.

With the bombing of Pearl Harbor, Alaska's backward infrastructure was recognized as a key strategic vulnerability, and billions of defense dollars arrived to build the Alaskan Highway and construct military bases and fortifications. By 1943, Alaska's population tripled to a quarter of a million but the vast majority were armed forces. After the war, the population

returned to about 100,000, only to swell again in the late 1940s as the Cold War sent new military personnel up north.

Hal Burt may well have been part of this new immigration. He was formerly W6U1K from California, but of course his new call number didn't have a W prefix as it was not yet a state of the Union.

In 1955, a constitutional convention admitted Alaska to the Union, and the state gained the prefix W7.

106—ZS3Z

Windhoek, South West Africa, is home to the Daan Viljoen Game Park teeming with gemsbok, blue wildebeest, and mountain zebra like the one on this card. Apparently, Reverend Jenkins celebrated New Year's Eve, 1949 on the air and spoke to Jerry just an hour before midnight. This sort of dedication to the hobby seems fairly typical.

108—HH5SS

This 1950 QSL from Stan Smith is printed on a postcard, a souvenir of the bicentennial exposition in Port-au-Prince, Haiti. It shows a crop of sisal plants at La Plantation Dauphine, which at the time was one of the world's largest and finest plantations. Sisal produces a tough fiber that is mainly used to make rope and twine, and when Stan worked there, Dauphine was a booming operation that had played a major role in World War II.

A Wall Street tycoon with fantasies of being a big plantation owner founded Dauphine in 1927. He was optimistic about the market for fiber, and, within a couple of decades, his holdings had grown to 13,500 acres. The plantation had a private railroad to traffic the crop from the fields to a modern plant that extracted the fiber. Stan and the other 4,000 employees lived in modern housing with a pool and a club house.

As World War II spread to the Philippines, supplies of manila hemp fiber disappeared and sisal demand skyrocketed to provide ropes for the US Navy. 12,000 workers cleared enough land to double the plantation. At the time of this QSL, La Plantation Dauphine was at its peak.

Within a few years, however, luck would change as new polypropylene fiber hit the market and replaced sisal twine. By the mid-1980s the plantation was surrendered to the Haitian government in lieu of taxes. Today, it sits in ruins.

112—ZD1SS

Sergeant Mann was Jerry's second contact with Freetown. By 1950, Sierra Leone had been a British protectorate for close to a century. The country had seen little development, serving mainly as a dumping ground for slaves until 1930, when diamonds were discovered. The former slaves or Creoles were originally from all parts of the continent and, having developed trade on the coast and assuming British ways, had begun to demand more of a political role after the war. Their independence from Britain, however, would not be granted until 1961.

The real power in the country stemmed from an agreement between the colonial authorities and the DeBeers mining company, a pact that gave away national mining and prospecting rights for 99 years. However, some hundred thousand foreign and illegal miners operated in the country, contributing to a general atmosphere of neglect and lawlessness. While two million carats of diamonds were pulled out of mines every year, virtually none of this enormous wealth has benefited the people of Sierra Leone.

118—W1MIQ

After more than two decades on the air, Jerry finally managed to work all the W call sign districts across the US. It is ironic that the last, elusive place he managed to contact was W1 in South Norwalk, just 36 miles from Hackensack.

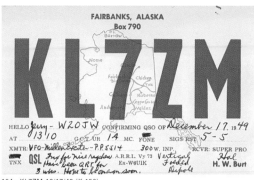

FAIRBANKS, ALASKA
Box 790

KL7ZM

HELLO *Jerry* – W2OJW CONFIRMING QSO OF *December 17,* 19 49
AT *0/3/0* GCT UR *14* MC. FONE SIGS RST *5-5*
XMTR: *VFO-Miller Xcycler-P.P.SS/4* 300 W. INP. RCVR: SUPER PRO
TNX QSL *Tnx for nice rigdow* A.R.R.L. Vy 73 *Vertical* *Hal*
Hav been QRS for Ex-W6U1K *Folded* H. W. Burt
3 whss. Hope to hr agn soon. *Dipole*

104—KL7ZM 12/17/49 (K:156)

FRENCH MOROCCO
GILBERT V. COLLIER
Navy 214, F. P. O., New York, N. Y., U. S. A.

CN8EL

RADIO *W2OJW* CONFIRMING QSO OF *24 DEC* 1949
AT *1945* GCT UR *14* MC FONE SIGS R *5* S *7* T
PSE QSL OM. TNX. Stateside W6MTH 73 GIL

105—CN8EL 12/24/49 (L:157)

108—HH5SS 1/17/50 (G:156)

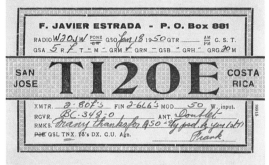

F. JAVIER ESTRADA – P. O. Box 881
RADIO *W2OJW* FONE QSO *Jan 18* 19 50 QTR AM PM C. S. T.
QSA *5* R *7* T — M — QRM — QRN — QSB — QRH — QRG *20* M

SAN JOSE # TI2OE COSTA RICA

XMTR *2-807's* FIN *2-616's* MOD *50* W. input.
RCVR *BC-348-0* ANT *Doublet*
RMKS: *Many thanks for QSO - vy gud to you 1st 11*
PSE QSL TNX. 73's DX. C.U. Agn. *Frank*

109—TI2OE 1/18/50 (H:156)

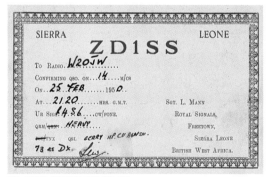

SIERRA LEONE
ZD1SS
To RADIO *W2OJW*
CONFIRMING QSO ON *14* M/cs
ON *25 FEB* 195 *0*
AT *21.20* HRS. G.M.T. SGT. L. MANN
UR SIGS *R4 S6* cw/FONE ROYAL SIGNALS,
QRM *HEAVY* FREETOWN,
TNX QSL *GERRY HP. CU AGN SN.* SIERRA LEONE
73 ES DX. *Len* BRITISH WEST AFRICA.

112—ZD1SS 2/25/50 (L:157) SEE 066

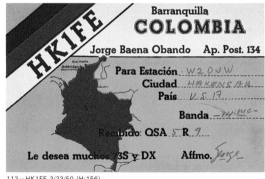

Barranquilla
COLOMBIA
Jorge Baena Obando Ap. Post. 134
Para Estación *W2 OJW*
Ciudad *HAKENSAK*
País *U. S. 17*
Banda *14 MC*
Recibido: QSA *5* R *9*
Le desea muchos 73S y DX Affmo. *Jorge*

113—HK1FE 3/23/50 (H:156)

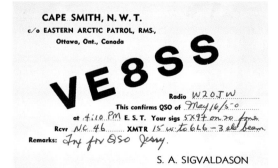

CAPE SMITH, N.W.T.
c/o EASTERN ARCTIC PATROL, RMS.,
Ottawa, Ont., Canada

VE8SS

Radio *W2OJW*
This confirms QSO of *May 16/s-0*
at *4:10 PM* E.S.T. Your sigs *5X9T on 20* fone
Rcvr *NC 46* XMTR *15 w to 616-3 el. beam*
Remarks: *Tnx for QSO Jerry.*

S. A. SIGVALDASON

116—VE8SS 5/16/50 (F:156)

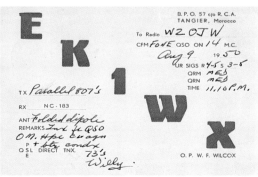

B. P. O. 57 c/o R.C.A.
TANGIER, Morocco
To Radio *W2OJW*
CFM FONE QSO ON *14* M.C.
Aug 9 19 *50*
UR SIGS R *4-5* S *3-5*
QRM *MED*
QRN *MED*
TIME *11.10 P.M.*
TX *Parallel 807's*
RX NC-183
ANT *Folded dipole*
REMARKS *Tnx fer QSO*
OM. Hpe cu agn
P + bte condx.
QSL DIRECT TNX.
73's
Willy.
O. P. W. F. WILCOX

117—EK1WX 8/9/50 (M:157) SEE 132

106—ZS3Z 12/31/49 (N:157)

107—KG6FI 1/4/50 (R:158) SEE 090

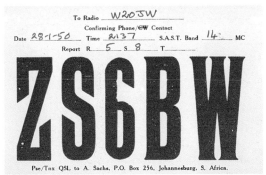

110—ZS6BW 1/28/50 (O:157)

111—SV0WI 2/25/50 (N:157)

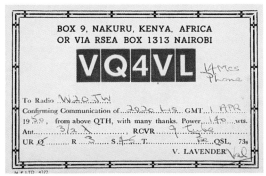

114—VQ4VL 4/1/50 (O:157)

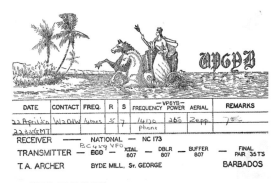

115—VP6YB 4/22/50 (H:156)

118—W1MIQ 8/12/50 (A:156)

119—K7FAH 8/14/50 (H:156)

Despite the defeat of Germany and Japan, world peace was still elusive. There was a growing threat that Communist China would intervene in the Korean War. The Iron Curtain came down across Eastern Europe, sealing it off from the Free World. The USSR successfully developed their own nuclear weapons. And in the US, McCarthy's Red Hunts added fuel to an atmosphere of fear and paranoia.

Hams were not immune; they feared that the Korean conflict would prompt the FCC to repeat the ruling that took them off the air during World War II. No such decision was made, but many of Jerry's calls in this period reflected the tension in global politics.

120—CN8EH 8/16/50 (L:157)

120—CN8EH

When the Korean War erupted and threatened World War III, Truman decided that Port Lyautey and its associated communications facilities did not provide enough US presence in North Africa. They decided to surround the USSR with a ring of strategic air bases, from Okinawa to Spain and Morocco.

NORTH KOREA FORCES INVADE SOUTH KOREA

PRESIDENT TRUMAN ORDERS US FORCES INTO KOREA

THE COSMOS

While Jerry sat at his radio in his basement, he was heavily influenced by cosmic events. Understanding the ways of the universe, of our solar system, of the cycle of the seasons, and conditions that vary each day and through each day, were all key to Jerry's getting the most out of his hobby.

At its most elementary, a radio signal travels on a path between two stations that can be connected by a straight line or a direct wave; this is called "line-of-sight" propagation. If it is uninterrupted, the signal can travel more or less to the visible horizon (FIG. 16). However, those waves can be bounced off something solid in the visible environment like a building, a mountain, or, if you've got enough power to transmit 222,000 miles, even the moon (FIG. 17).

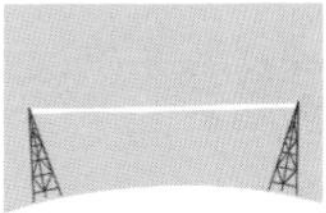

At a different frequency, radio signals can also pass along the ground, traveling over that mountain rather than bouncing off it and can go beyond the visible horizon (FIG. 18). Of course, the composition and temperature of the surface has a lot of impact on those waves and how far and how strongly they carry. But even under the best conditions, like when the earth and air are full of water, Jerry didn't reach the South Pacific with ground waves.

He used the sky as his refractor by transmitting signals up through the Earth's atmosphere. Above the stratosphere, from 25 to 400 miles above the ground, lie electrically charged bands collectively known as the ionosphere. These layers, ionized by the sun's ultraviolet radiation, function as mirrors of different densities to bend signals back to the Earth from below. Depending on their height and permeability, these ringed bands can ricochet radio signals thousands of miles around the globe (FIG. 19). The ionosphere is affected by temperature, season, sun spots, meteors, distance, and a host of factors that make ham radio an unpredictable and exciting adventure.

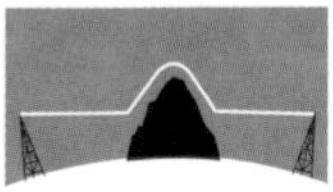

The rich stew of atmospheric factors means that nearby signals can be overwhelmed by distant ones, that new stations can be picked up where they were never heard before, that new doors are opened, new horizons crossed. The atmosphere functions like a mirrored ball bouncing light around a dance floor. Knowing how to focus and control that refraction is a technical art shaped by experience and luck.

FIG. 16
Line of sight

FIG. 17
Bounce

FIG. 18
Ground waves

At one time of year, a certain frequency may be absorbed by the ionosphere while another passes clear through it to disappear into deep space, and yet a third is perfectly refracted back to Earth thousands of miles from its transmitter and picked up with great clarity. Six months later, the first frequency will bounce off the ionosphere instead of being absorbed and the third will disappear, winging its way deeper and deeper out into the cosmos.

Like any seasoned operator, Jerry knew a great deal about each layer of the atmosphere and how it would propagate under different conditions. He charted the 11-year cycles of sunspots, which are the strongest influencer of ionization. He knew that ionization was lowest just before dawn so while his family was still tucked in bed, he was in his ham shack, working the airwaves.

Like many DXers, Jerry favored the 20-meter HF band. When sunspots are low and a signal can penetrate much of the ionosphere, the doors to great distance are open around the clock. When the sun had set on Hackensack, he could aim his antenna west and catch the sunshine over the Pacific or aim east where the sun was rising and charging the ionosphere into a refracting dome over Eastern Europe.

When the conditions were right, he'd be reaching through the lower layers of the ionosphere and up hundreds of miles above the Earth to the F layer, where he could skip 20 MHz signals that traveled thousands of miles.

In the summer, when the sun is closer and the rays are more direct, the ionization increases. However, during daytime, that ionization can surge to a point where the F layer can be split into two layers, each of which is less ionized than a typical midwinter combined F layer. Suddenly great conditions could lose their refractive power and fill Jerry's speakers with static and hiss. And, on a clear midwinter night, completely new parts of the world would come in that were unreachable in the summer.

Weather fronts can also affect propagation. The lowest layer of the Earth's atmosphere is called the troposphere and its fronts can bend and duct radio signals above 30 MHz.

Other cosmic events can effect propagation too. Small meteors regularly enter the Earth's atmosphere. As they burn up, they create an

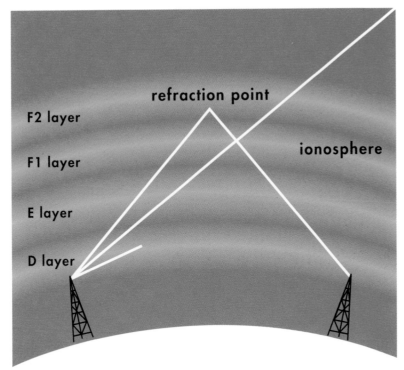

refraction point

F2 layer

ionosphere

F1 layer

E layer

D layer

FIG. 19

Long distance radio
propagation

**The ionosphere can act like a wall,
an open door, or a mirror.**

ionized trail that can be a great refractor. Hams anticipate meteor showers—sending out regular 15- to 30-second bursts of signals to take advantage of the irregular bonanza of cosmic debris. While they don't allow for sustained ragchewing, they can function as a sort of flare that establishes valid contact between extremely remote stations operating at lower frequencies like 50 MHz. Hams refer to a meteor that produces a particularly long signal as a "blue whizzer."

The auroras over the poles are also heavily charged and are used as refractors to bounce signals long distances. These forces and the strong magnetic pull of the poles often influenced Jerry's contacts with hams in the Arctic.

WHY

ARE RADIO AMATEURS

called

"HAMS"

FOUR EXPLANATIONS

(pick one):

In G. M. Dodge's classic book on wire telegraphy, *The Telegraph Instructor*, published in 1908 before amateur radio began, the term is defined as "a poor operator," or a "plug." In the early days of wireless, former landline operators brought their skills, traditions, and vocabulary to the new technology. When they collided with eager new ham-fisted amateurs in the crowded airwaves, they would derisively refer to them as "hams," which the amateurs, possibly in ignorance, assumed for themselves with pride. In a similar way, computer programmers have adopted terms like "geek," "nerd," and "hacker" to identify their own community.

A variation on this theory has it that early British shipboard operators, when complaining about amateur interference, pronounced the term with an "h," "hamateurs," which was ultimately shortened to "ham."

An acronym for "Help All Mankind."

In the early days when operators chose their own call letters, three members of the Harvard Radio Club used their initials H, A, and M to identify themselves. This station became famous and ultimately synonymous with amateur radio when it was used as an example to oppose the 1911 Wireless Regulation Bill, which would have controlled such amateur activity out of existence.

HAM CLUBS

Ham radio is not just a solitary, on-air hobby. The amateur radio community organizes many special social events for operators and their families. Announcements of parties; tailgates; flea markets; swap meets; hamfests; and state, regional, and national hamventions fill their magazines and websites.

There are more than 2,000 ham radio clubs across the US. At their meetings, speakers report on technology advances and regulation issues, discuss emergency services and gear, review radio history, present videos of their DXpeditions, and do a lot of in-person ragchewing. When friends who have just met over the radio have face-to-face contact, they hand out business-size cards called "eyeball QSLs," a souvenir of their meeting. Clubs also provide many community services. They send speakers to encourage the hobby among school children and scouts, and provide support for parades, marathons, and air and boat shows. They also develop special drills and field days to prepare for supporting the community in case of emergencies.

Jerry and Mabel attended many club meetings and outings. He was very active in the Quarter Century Wireless Association (QCWA), a club comprised of hams with at least 25 years of on-air experience, eventually serving as president of his chapter.

FIG. 20

Jerry and other members of the QCWA

30 Town News, December 29, 1982

'Elmer Of Year' Award Is Presented

Gerald Powell of Oradell, president of the Northern N.J. Chapter of given by the Federal Communications Commission before they Milford, and Joe Pettengill, N2BC of Rutherford.

HONORED - Left to right, Quarter Century Wireless Association members Joe Pettengill [N2BC], G. Powell [W20JW], F. Burns [W2Kww] and J. Slack [W2BLQ.]

the Quarter Century Wireless Association and operator of amateur radio station W20JW, presented the "Elmer of the Year" award to Francis Leonard, W2NTP of Fair Lawn, during the chapter's annual dinner meeting at the Robin Hood in Clifton.

An "Elmer" is an experienced "ham" radio operator who distinguishes himself by giving generously and gratuitously of his time and talent to help new, would-be operators, by teaching them the morse code and electronic theory

needed to pass the rigorous examinations will grant an amateur license.

The "Elmer" does not stop there, however. He also assists the newly licensed-operators to set up their stations, improve their proficiency, troubleshoot, and to acquire good operating practices.

Certificates evidencing 50 years of continuous amateur operation were also awarded by Powell to John Slack, W2BLQ, of River Edge, Gordon Gregory, N2IN, of Denville, Frederick Burns, W2KWW, of New

QUARTER CENTURY WIRELESS ASSOCIATION, INC.

THE QUARTER CENTURY WIRELESS ASSOCIATION INC.

presents this

70th Anniversary Award

to its

Distinguished Member

GERALD POWELL

W2OJW

to commemorate

Seventy Years of Service

as a Licensed Radio Amateur

_____
General Manager

_____
President

Until the 1960s, the FCC required that all amateurs keep a detailed log of their on-air activities. Each contact had to be described in detail and the logs preserved for at least a year in case of a later complaint and investigation. FCC regulation 97.103 required the address and signature of the operator, the type of emission, the input power to the final amplifier, the frequency band used, the call sign of the station called, the message traffic handled, the location of the station at the time of the call (which could change if the operator was calling mobile), and the data and time of contact.

FIG. 23

Cartoon, 1949.
QST Magazine.
"OM" is an acronym
for "old man," a
common greeting
between hams.

While the regulation has been relaxed, most hams still note every call they make, and the log has evolved to become a ham's journal. They also use it to record changes to their gear: new equipment acquired, the changes they made to their circuits, variations in their antenna systems, problems, and solutions. Next to each QSO, they record if and when they sent off QSLs in response. Logs are also useful for recalling previous contacts with a particular ham, recording noteworthy calls, and providing substantiation for awards.

The old notebooks have been replaced by computer and Palm Pilot databases that can be shared on the Internet. The ARRL has developed the Logbook of the World, a system to cross-reference logbooks to substantiate contacts and automate the awards process.

Aklavik emerged from obscurity as a trapping community in 1932 when Albert Johnson, "the Mad Trapper of Rat River" shot a Mountie and then escaped into the snow. For the first time, law enforcement used airplanes and radio to track a criminal,

but the hunt took 42 days. Before he was caught, shot, and buried in Aklavik, Johnson managed to survive in the winter wilderness with no supplies or dogs, to take down several other Mounties, and become a coast-to-coast celebrity.

At the time of this contact, Aklavik was in the spotlight again. Rapid development had melted the permafrost and caused severe flooding so the government planned to relocate everyone and abandon the town. Many residents of Aklavik refused to move,

rallying around the hamlet's symbol: a picture of a beaver under the motto "Never Say Die." To generate support and stimulate development, children wrote and sung protest songs, which generated nationwide support and saved the town.

121—VK5OD 8/26/50 (R:158)

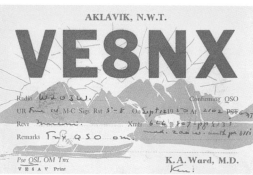

122—VE8NX 9/12/50 (J:156)

123—CR7AH 9/15/50 (O:157)

124—ZS4AZ/ZS4AX 12/2/50 (O:157)

125—KR6FA 12/12/50 (Q:158) SEE 097, 145, 273

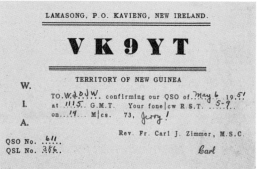

126—VK9YT 5/6/51 (R:158)

Dale was probably getting ready to ship out
of Tokyo after six years of American occupation. In just three weeks, 49 nations would
sign the Japanese peace treaty in San
Francisco.

Japan was devastated at the end of the war;
it was primarily a rural country that relied on
traditional methods and had little
or no public health, modern sanitation, or
proper industry. Under the Allied occupation,
the country was rebuilt and a democratic
government established. Before long, it
would become one of the world's dominant
industrial powers.

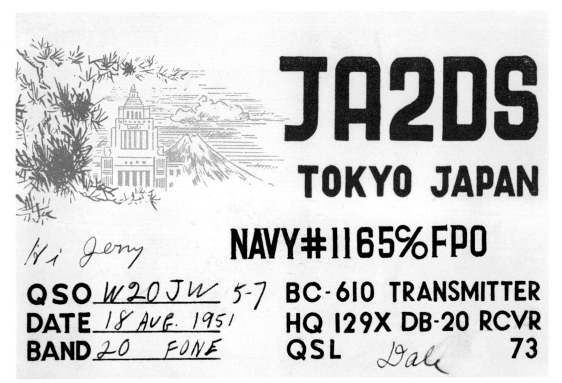

127—JA2DS 8/18/51 (Q:158)

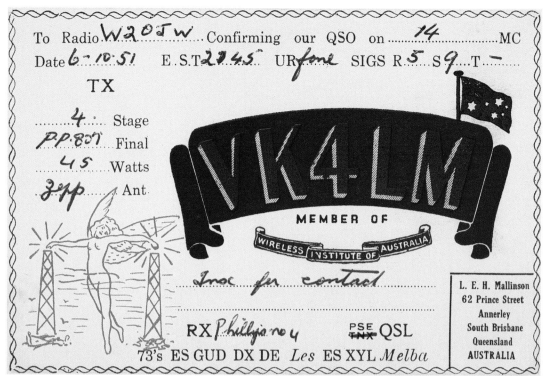

To Radio W2OJW Confirming our QSO on 14 MC
Date 6-10-51 E.S.T 22.45 UR fone SIGS R 5 S 9 T —

TX

4 Stage
P.P.807 Final
45 Watts
2pp Ant

VK4LM

MEMBER OF

WIRELESS INSTITUTE OF AUSTRALIA

Tnsc fr contact

RX Phillips no 4   PSE TNX QSL

73's ES GUD DX DE Les ES XYL Melba

L. E. H. Mallinson
62 Prince Street
Annerley
South Brisbane
Queensland
AUSTRALIA

128—VK4LM 10/6/51 (R:158)

COLOR TV INTRODUCED

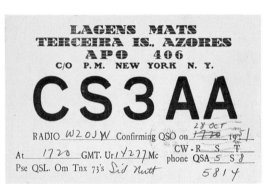

129—CS3AA 10/28/51 (K:157)

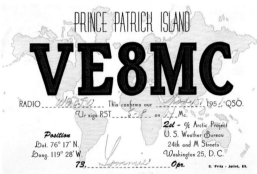

130—VE8MC 11/17/51 (J:156) SEE 081, 089, 141, 149, 151

131—W0BHP & W0VQC 1/23/52 (G:156)

132—KT1DD 5/1/52 (M:157) SEE 117

131—W0BHP & W0VQC

Mr. and Mrs. Frank Curtis, Jr.
were both licensed amateurs
in Virgil, South Dakota
(current population: 33).

This is Jerry's first contact with a Japanese citizen, less than a year after occupation ended.

Hirosaki seems to be an appropriate place to begin a new peace. The city's emblem is the *gmanji,* or reversed swastika, a symbol of the rejection of selfish motives and the devotion of the individual to society. The town managed to avoid serious damage during the war and emerged as a center of culture and education as well as home of Japan's finest apple orchards.

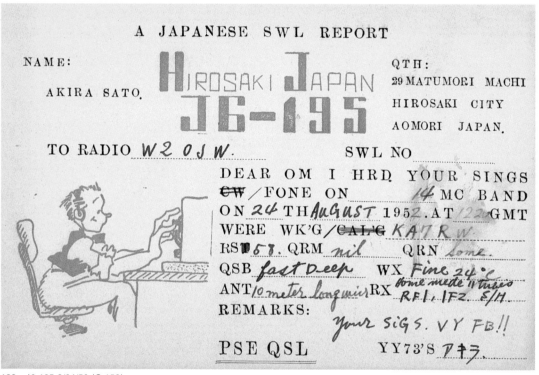

133—J6-195 8/24/52 (Q:158)

134—VP3YG

"On the Route of the Flying Clippers" is a reference to Pan Am's famed flying boats.

Only the wealthiest travelers could afford a ticket, many of which ran to three times an average annual salary, but the accommodations were as luxurious as an ocean liner's and the speed was unrivaled.

In 1934, the Clippers began a six-day route from Miami to Buenos Aires, hopping between fueling stops and passing over Desmond Yong and his neighbors in British Guiana. By 1952, however, the days of the Clipper were over, rendered obsolete by the new aviation technology developed during the war.

137—KV4AA

Dick Spenceley was one of the legends of amateur radio. Until his key went silent in 1982, he was on the air with hams around the world for 55 years.

In 1925, he joined the US Navy radio station in St. Thomas and became a ham in 1927. He went on to become one of the world's highest scoring contest DXers in the 1950s and, in 1962, capped the DXCC Honor Roll. From 1952 to 1958, he was DX Editor of *CQ*, the leading amateur magazine, and was inducted into the CQ DX Hall of Fame in 1969.

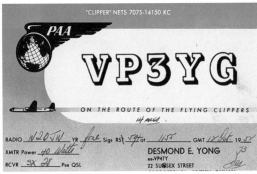

134—VP3YG 10/12/52 (I:156)

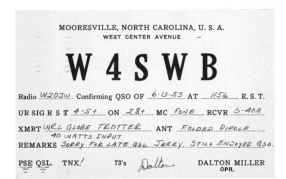

135 W4SWB 6/13/53 (C:156)

136 PY8MV 9/7/53 (L:156)

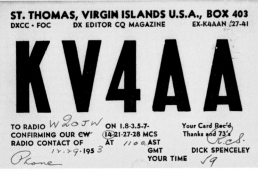

137—KV4AA 12/29/53 (H:156)

139—KX6AF

This is the third QSL card
from KX6AF depicting the
US Navy base on Kwajelein
Atoll and the ham shack
with its massive antenna.

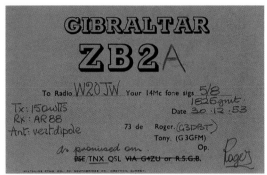

138—ZB2A 12/30/53 (M:157)

KX6AF

Kwajalein   M. I.

139—KX6AF 8/2/54 (R:158) SEE 071, 155, 156

140—5A2TZ 1/9/55 (M:157)

141—W1KGH-VE8 3/5/55 (G-156) SEE 089, 130, 149, 151, 186

142—KG1AA

Greenland is the largest island in the world, but 85 percent of the land is covered in solid icepack that is a 100,000 years old and over a mile thick. Appropriately, it was of enormous strategic importance during the Cold War. The air base was designed to supply and refuel long-range bombers on their way to take out Moscow.

On the bottom of the card is a reference to MARS, the Military Affiliate Radio System, which began in 1925 when the army began recruiting hams to help develop military radio technology and train soldiers in communications. Today, it continues to support radio, an extracurricular activity for servicemen, and to provide communications support in case of emergency.

143—4X4CK

This QSL was a rare accomplishment for Jerry: Chaim was one of only a few Israeli radio amateurs in 1955. Only seven years after its founding, Israel was still a struggling country, and its operators had enormous difficulties getting equipment and parts.

142—KG1AA 5/29/55 (H:156) SEE 238

143—4X4CK 6/30/55 (N:157)

144—KA0IJ 7/1/55 (Q:158) SEE 298

CHURCHILL RESIGNS

OKINAWA AMATEUR RADIO CLUB
APO 331, San Francisco, Calif.

KR6AF

OKINAWA

Radio Station _W2OJw_ Confirm QSO _8 July_ 195 _5_ AT _20:35_
UR SIG ^{Fone} R _5_ S _9_ T₀ _9_ Power _800 Watts_
Rec. _57-J_ Xmitter _450 Final_ Ant _3 El Beam_

Remarks_____

~~TNX,~~ PLSE QSL — 73'S _Bill and gang._

145—KR6AF 7/8/55 (Q:158) SEE 097, 125, 273

113

7/55

Henry was a member of the
USAF Airways and Air
Communications Service,
which provided air-to-ground
and ground-to-air communications for the air force. He dealt
with crypto, teletype, message
center, and radio operations.

146—KA5HM 7/15/55 (Q:158)

145—KR6AF (BACK)

JOHNSTON ISLAND
MID PACIFIC

JOHN J. HALSER OPR.
A P O 105
SAN FRANCISCO, CALIF.

KJ6FAA

GREETING TO _W2OJW_ TNX FOR QSO OF _JULY 18_ 19 _55_
AT _0130_ LOCAL TIME. ON _14_ MC.
UR ~~PHONE~~ SIGS WERE R _5_ S _9_ T ____
XMITTER _ART-13_ ANT _LONG WIRE_
QSL TNX   73 JACK

147—KJ6FAA 7/18/55 (M:155) SEE 159

CONSTRUCTION

COLONIZATION

Roy S. LeTourneau

Seek ye the Lord while he may be found, call ye upon him while he is near.—Isaiah 55:6

OA3L

LeTourneau del Peru, Inc.
Tournavista, Peru

148—OA3L 7/21/55 (J:156)

PERONE OUSTED IN ARGENTINA

The LeTourneau family were extremely successful as "God's businessmen" with a dual commitment to the gospel and to construction equipment. Ray's father, Robert G. LeTourneau, introduced the rubber tire into the earthmoving and material handling industry, developed huge mobile offshore drilling platforms, and employed three full-time chaplains in his manufacturing plants. He also traveled the world as a missionary.

In 1953, after building a successful mission in Liberia, R. G. LeTourneau began planning a colony in Peru. In a deal with the government he built 31 miles of the Trans-Andean Highway that would link the Amazon and the Pacific. In exchange, he received a million acres deep in the jungle. The site was extremely inaccessible, and the company built a 4,600-mile supply route from Vickburg, Mississippi to the mouth of the Amazon and onto the new village of Tournavista.

As the river was plagued by sandbars, Robert developed a walking ship, the Lizzie Lorimer, with four keels and propellers that let it move across areas where water was, as one sailor described, "no deeper than the dew." He also developed new lumbering equipment to work deep in the dense rain forest.

Tournavista's mission was fourfold: to supply the local people with machinery and train them to use it; to establish a model village with electricity, airport, hospital, school, church, and ham radio station; to clear the land for farming; and to teach the gospel and train local pastors. The goal was to make the colony self-sustaining, no longer dependent on shipments from abroad. By 1960, 5,000 acres were under production, and the town had a population of 500.

Tournavista became a center for mission work. Missionaries vacationed there, and local children attended its school. The farm was very productive; cattle were brought in all the way from the LeTourneau ranch in Texas. Robert went on to establish the LeTourneau University in Longview, Texas and to write his memoirs, *Mover of Men and Mountains*. He passed away in 1969.

Roy continues to spread the word. He is the founder of several ministries and former chairman of the international board of the Christian Businessmen's Committee.

Tournavista still exists as a tiny colony deep in the Amazon but details of its current condition are sketchy.

Newfoundland

ERNEST HARMON AFB

W1FVB/VO4

Radio _W2OSW_ This confirms Ur ___ Mc. ᶠᴼᴺᴱ/CW sigs RST ___ 57+

our _11 Dec_ 195_, QSO. at _0915_ 75 m. GMT.

Xmtr: _32U1_ Ant: _2 elem_ Rcvr: _HQ-129X_

MARS RADIO STATION
BOX 235

AJ9AL "73" STEPHENVILLE, NFLD.
Operator "JOE"
"JERRY"

C. Fritz · Joliet, Ill.

149—W1FVB/VO4 11/12/55 (E:156) SEE 089, 130, 141, 151

124°W 72°N BANKS ISLAND

VE8OY

RADIO _W2OJW_ This confirms our _Jany 8_ 195_6_, QSO.

Collins 32V1 Ur sigs RST _5 S 7/9_ on _14_ Mc. phone _1300 GMT_

Hammarlund 129X
Telrex 3 el beam

2sl - Thomas T. Joines
via Chas H. Harris VE6HM
10806-125 St Edmonton
Alta.

73. _Tommie_ Opr.

C. Fritz · Joliet, Ill.

Printed in USA

151—VE8OY 1/8/56 (J:156) SEE 089, 130, 141, 149

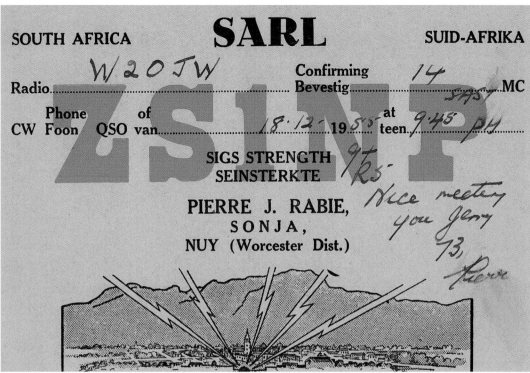

SOUTH AFRICA   **SARL**   **SUID-AFRIKA**

Radio ___W2OJW___ Confirming Bevestig ___14___ MC

Phone of
CW Foon QSO van ___18.12.19 55___ at teen ___9.45 pм___

SIGS STRENGTH
SEINSTERKTE ___9t R5___

PIERRE J. RABIE,
SONJA,
NUY (Worcester Dist.)

Nice meeting you Jerry 73, Pierre

150—ZS1NP 12/18/55 (O:157)

HEADQUARTERS
6101st M & S GROUP.
APO 157 San Francisco, Calif.

KA3KB

To ___W2OJW___ Confirming QSO of ___14 March___ at ___2100___ hrs. Japan Time
On ___14 7ммc___ MC. UR sigs RST ___5 9___ Ant. ___4El Beam___
Rcvr ___BC-779___ Xmtr ___Viking KW___ W. Input ___1000___

PSE QSL Tnx 73 *Russ W2HPD*

152—KA3KB 3/24/56 (Q:158)

There's an interesting parenthetic note under this quote from Romans 1:16: For FB ("fine business" or "good quality") QSO ("contact") with Heaven, read all of Romans.

154-CR6AI

Joåo Carlos Chaves was Portuguese, though his ancestors had been in Angola for half a millennium. The Portuguese first came to Angola in the late fifteenth century; instead of gold, they found the local Bantus and tapped them as a source of slave labor for their Brazilian colonies. Over a million Liberians were enslaved before Portugal lost Brazil in 1836. Though illegal, the Liberian slave trade persevered until the early twentieth century.

Beyond dumping its own criminals as colonists, known as *degredados*, Portugal did next to nothing to develop the infrastructure of the country for centuries.

After World War II, Portugal finally began investing in its colony, helping to harness hydroelectric power and to develop industry. Coffee, diamond, and oil exports strengthened the economy, and many new settlers arrived from the motherland, soon making up five percent of the country's population. Despite the authorities' professed aim of multiracial equality, Africans were repressed and did not share in the billions of dollars of wealth being pulled out of their land. Nationalists were not offered even the possibility of independence and could not organize openly.

Joåo lived in a repressive and depressing place that was still at relative peace in 1950 when this contact took place. Before long it would erupt into a vicious and prolonged civil war that would drag in the world's superpowers and last for the rest of the century.

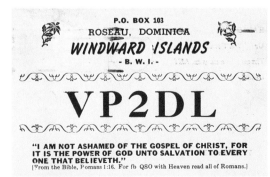

153—VP2DL 3/24/56 (H:156)

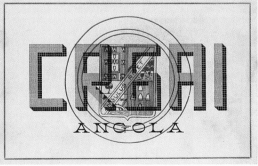

154—CR6AI 5/4/56 (N:157)

155—KX6AF 6/25/56 (R:158) SEE 071, 139, 156

FIRST AERIAL H-BOMB
—EQUIVALENT TO TEN MILLION
TONS OF TNT TESTED OVER BIKINI
ATOLL IN PACIFIC OCEAN

This was the navy's ham shack on Kwaj (see also 071—KX6AF), close to the site where the US had just begun conducting aerial nuclear tests. The first had occurred just a month before when an H-bomb equivalent to ten million tons of TNT was detonated over Namu islet on the Bikini Atoll.

Operators on Kwaj reported seeing the detonation of another megaton thermonuclear device over Johnston Island, some 1,500 miles away. A rainbow-shaped arc of white light appeared at the horizon and reflected off the surface of the Pacific, growing in intensity as the men watched it for 15 minutes. The hams heard the radio signal on 20 meters snap off as if dead and then return half an hour later and warble with a strange Doppler effect. The bomb had created enormous turbulence in the ionosphere. No report on what it did to the men watching it from Kwaj.

"THE PEARL
OF THE PACIFIC"

KWAJALEIN
KX6BU

MARSHALL ISLANDS

U. S. NAVAL AMATEUR RADIO STATION

NAVY 824   BOX 3

FPO SAN FRANCISCO, CAL.

KH6AU PRINT

73 _Joe_ W5JTQ OPERATOR   _____QSL

156—KX6BU 6/30/56 (R:158) SEE 071, 139, 155

MOROCCO GAINS INDEPENDENCE

This handmade card from a sailor uses a phonetic alphabet peculiar to the US Navy of the period:

Able Baker Charlie Dog Easy Fox George How Item Jig King Love Mike Nan Oboe Peter Queen Roger Sugar Tare Uncle Victor William X-ray Yoke Zebra.

The ARRL alphabet of the period would have spelled out the call letters as: King Mary Six Frank Adam Adam.

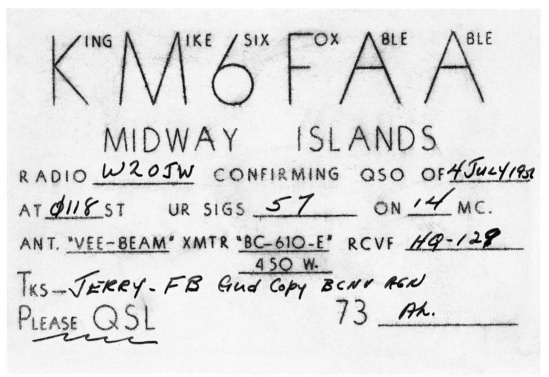

157—KM6FAA 7/4/56 (M:155)

159—KJ6AW 7/5/56 (M:155) SEE 147

158—KX6BP

Apparently, Jerry spent the Fourth of July speaking to servicemen in the South Pacific (see also 157—KM6FAA). This club of air force men on the "Land o' Coconut Crabs and Killer Clams" had already incorporated the atomic tests into their QSL card design.

159—KJ6AW

This card has no return address, date, or details of the contact. It appears to be from the 1950s.

The legend on the sign behind this group of servicemen reads "Sand Isle. Pop. 6 men. 1 dog. Elev. 7. Never has (sic) so few been inspected by so many."

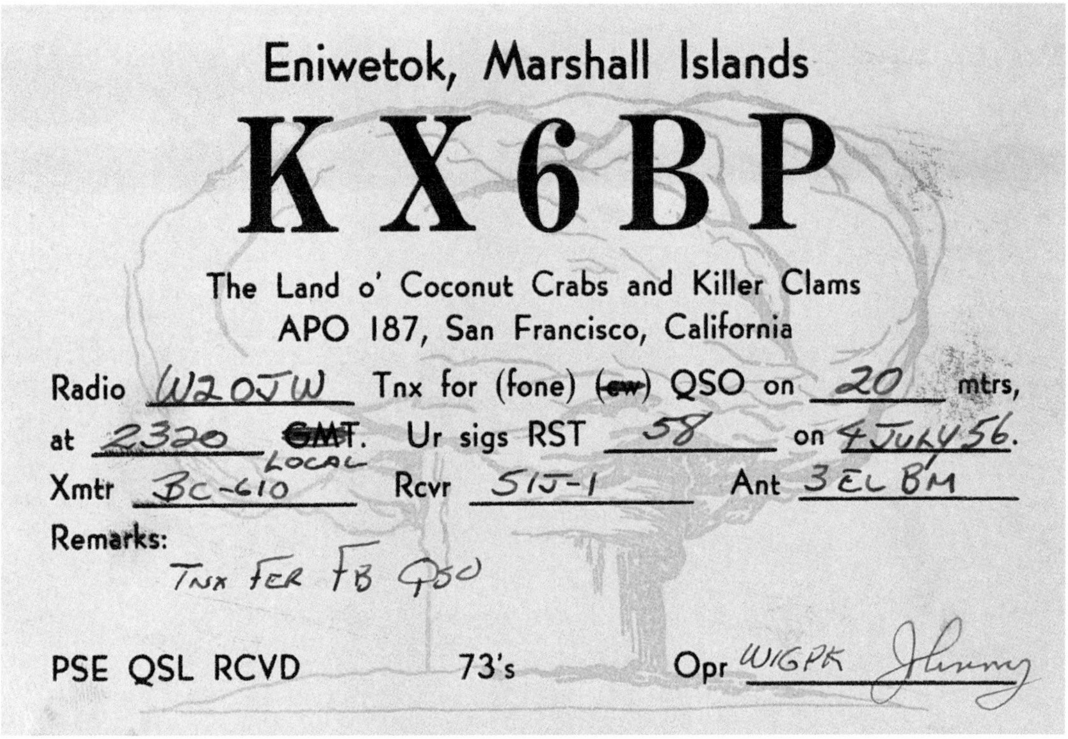

Eniwetok, Marshall Islands
KX6BP

The Land o' Coconut Crabs and Killer Clams
APO 187, San Francisco, California

Radio _W2OJW_ Tnx for (fone) (cw) QSO on _20_ mtrs,
at _2320_ ~~GMT~~. Ur sigs RST _58_ on _4 JULY 56_.
        LOCAL
Xmtr _BC-610_ Rcvr _51J-1_ Ant _3 EL BM_

Remarks:
Tnx fer FB QSO

PSE QSL RCVD   73's   Opr _W16PK_ _Jimmy_

158—KX6BP 7/4/56 (R:158) SEE 161

Long before the advent of cell phones, Doc Parker, "the Radio Hack," contacted Jerry from a mobile radio from his car as he crossed the George Washington Bridge, not far from Hackensack. The doc's card is a ham's delight. In one corner the stork wears radio headphones while delivering a baby. In the other, Franconia's greatest treasure, the natural formation of Conway red granite known as "the Old Man of the Mountain" is also sporting a set of cans.

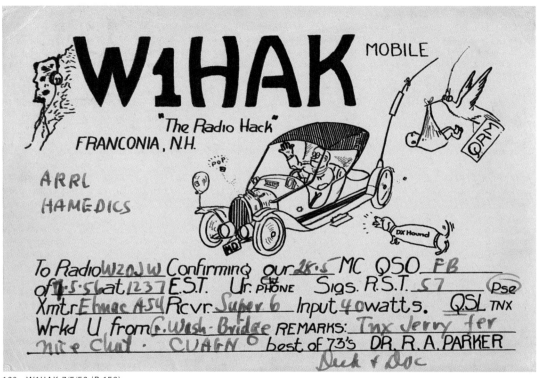

160—W1HAK 7/5/56 (B:156)

Another call to KX6BP but this time, Jerry connected with a completely different ham at the radio set.

Eniwetok, Marshall Islands

KX6BP

The Land o' Coconut Crabs and Killer Clams
APO 187, San Francisco, California

Radio W2OJW Tnx for (fone) (cw) QSO on 20 mtrs,

at 2350 GMT. Ur sigs RST 59 on 15 JULY 56

Xmtr BC 610 Rcvr COLLINS 51J. Ant 3 EL. BEAM

Remarks:

PSE QSL RCVD   73's   Opr WS BVX "JEEP"

161—KX6BP 7/15/56 (M:155) SEE 158

162—VK6RU

Jim Rumble was an important Australian ham until his death in 1999. He was often at the top of the DXCC roles and served as QSL manager of his region for over 60 years. As a testament to his contributions, the Western Australian division of the Wireless Institute of Australia renamed their biggest honor the "Jim Rumble Amateur of the Year Award."

164—KH6UL

This contact is with the club station at NAVCAMS EAST-PAC, the navy's communications facility in the middle of Oahu, near the town of Wahiawa.

167—W3MUK/VO1

Argentia Naval Base was the most expensive US base built in World War II, strategically positioned to patrol and protect the North Atlantic. Tens of thousands of military and civilian employees were stationed at Argentia throughout the conflict. Aircraft from its airstrip escorted convoys and trawled for submarines and U-boats. In 1941, Churchill and Roosevelt came to the Ship Harbor anchorage for their historic Atlantic Charter meeting.

After World War II, the air force and then the navy maintained the base. Steven Eldridge was part of the navy's Air Logistics Center, but by 1957 the Korean War was over and the number of personnel had been drastically reduced.

In the mid-1970s, the base was disestablished and returned to the Canadians, who were left to spend a hundred million dollars to deal with the PCB barrels and the after effects of the nuclear weapons that were stored at Argentia.

169—VR2BJ

This is the second (see also 073) QSL card that Jerry received from Malcolm Gray in Suva, Fiji. The design of the card has changed very radically: Gray surprinted his call letters in sunset pink onto a photo postcard (printed in England) and moved all of his contact information to the back of the card.

USSR LAUNCHES SPUTNIK, THE FIRST MAN-MADE SATELLITE

VK6RU

Many thanks for the ___ Mc
Phone CW contact of ___ at
___ W.A.S.T. Your signals were RST ___

DXCC

WAP   WAS   WAZ   WAC
PSE TKS QSL

JIM RUMBLE
15 THE GROVE
WEMBLEY
WEST AUSTRALIA

162—VK6RU 8/4/56 (R:158)

BENALLA, VICTORIA
AUSTRALIA
VK3AIL

To Radio _W2OJW_   Confirming QSO of _26. Aug, 1956_

At _21/53_ E.A.S.T. UR _14_ MC   FONE SIGS R _5_ S _8_ T —

Ant. _2λ_   TX _50 watts_ RX _home made_

73, "LEX," ARMY CANTEEN SERVICE, BENALLA.

163—VK3AIL 8/26/56 (R:158)

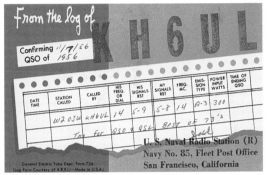

From the log of

KH6UL

Confirming _11/7/56_
QSO of _1956_

DATE TIME	STATION CALLED	CALLED BY	HIS FREQ. OR DIAL	HIS SIGNALS RST	MY SIGNALS RST	FREQ. MC.	EMIS- SION TYPE	POWER INPUT WATTS	TIME OF ENDING QSO
	W2OJW	KH6UL	14	5-9	5-8	14	A-3	300	
	Tnx for QSO & QSL				Best of 73's				

General Electric Tube Dept. Form 73A
(Log Form Courtesy of A.R.R.L.)—Made in U.S.A.

U. S. Naval Radio Station (R)
Navy No. 85, Fleet Post Office
San Francisco, California

164—KH6UL 11/7/58 (L:155) SEE 273

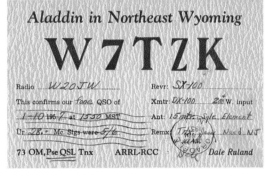

Aladdin in Northeast Wyoming
W7TZK

Radio _W2OJW_   Revr: _SX-100_

This confirms our _fone_ QSO of   Xmtr: _DX-100_ 200 W. input

_1-10-195 7_ at _1550_ MST   Ant: _15 mtr. Sgle. Element_

Ur _28.7_ Mc Sigs were _5/6_   Remx:

73 OM, Pse QSL Tnx   ARRL-RCC   Dale Ruland

165—W7TZK 1/10/57 (G:156)

★ ST. ALBANS, VERMONT ★

K1AXO

Radio _W2OJW_ QSO of _Nov 11_ 1957
_28_ Mc fone sigs _5T 5-9_ at _120_ E.S.T.
_DX100_   Revr: _RME 4300_
TNX.   _Bud_

166—K1AXO 11/11/57 (B:156)

ARGENTIA, NEWFOUNDLAND

W3MUK/VO1

AREC
ARRL
RCC

PSE QSL:

Roscoe "Steve" Eldridge, ALC, U. S. N.
772 Pine Lane, Clermont, Florida

167—W3MUK/VO1 12/23/57 (F:156)

SWAN ISLAND
WEST INDIES

W4IHW/KS4

Home QTH
3991 N. W. 65 AVE.
MIAMI SPRINGS, FLORIDA

I. H. VOSBRINK
"VOS"

168—W4IHW/KS4 1/19/58 (H:156)

VR2BJ

FIJIAN BURE AND LAGOON, CUVU

PHOTO BY BOLTON STINSON

169—VR2BJ 6/6/58 (R:158)

171 — K4TLN

Glenn Murphy contacted Jerry from Athens, Alabama on November 28, 1959. His card shows pictures of his family: Mark, Karen, and his XYL (wife). On the back of the card he makes a remark that suggests Jerry was an "Elmer," or a mentor, to young hams learning the ropes: "Say hi to Pete and the other boy, didn't get his handle." Glenn has reconstructed the map of the US on his wall.

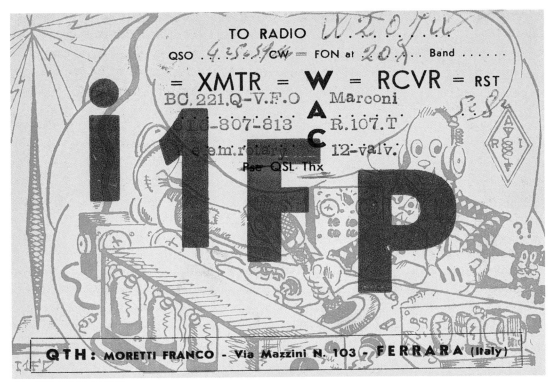

170—I1FP 4/25/59 (M:157)

171—K4TLN 11/28/59 (E:156)

FUKUOKA JAPAN

EX-W4ROT

JA7RW

ROY A WHISTLE 1ST LT USAF
APO ~~929~~ 163-1 SAN FRANCISCO

172—JA7RW 10/10/63 (Q:158)

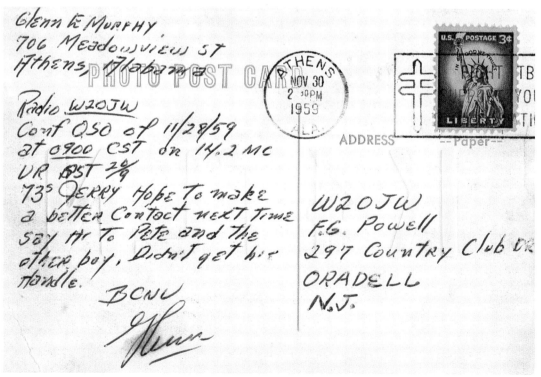

Glenn E. Murphy,
706 Meadowview St
Athens, Alabama

Radio W2OJW
Conf QSO of 11/28/59
at 0900 CST on 14.2 MC
UR RST 2/9
73s Jerry Hope To make
a better Contact next Time
Say Hi To Pete and the
other boy, Didn't get his
Handle.
BCNU

PHOTO POST CARD

ATHENS
NOV 30
2 30PM
1959
ALA.

ADDRESS   --Paper--

U.S. POSTAGE 3¢
LIBERTY

W2OJW
F.G. Powell
297 Country Club Dr
ORADELL
N.J.

171—K4TLN (BACK)

172—JA7RW

Fukuoka is the Japanese gateway to China and Southeast Asia. From Kublai Khan's invasion in the thirteenth century to the hammering it took during World War II, Fukuoka has ushered in many significant influences on Japan's history and culture. Just 70 miles from Korea, it also played a vital role in the Cold War.

US airmen like Lieutenant Whistle were stationed at the Itazuke airbase and launched many bombing and all-weather squadrons across the Yellow Sea to Korea. Nuclear weapons are alleged to have been stored in the hills of Hakata-no-mori. In January 1954, another bombshell was dropped on Fukoaka, when MPs from the base were called in to control crowds gathered to see Marilyn Monroe and Joe DiMaggio on their honeymoon at the Kokusai Hotel.

173—HI4ARM

On this QSL from the Dominican Republic, Rafael makes the handwritten notation: "Have bananas, will ship."

174—PJ5ME

A two-day DXpedition of seven members of the Connecticut Wireless Association to Saint Martin in the Dutch Antilles.

173—HI4ARM 9/10/64 (G:156)

174—PJ5ME 3/27/66 (H:156)

FIRST COMMUNICATIONS SATEL-
LITE PUT IN ORBIT

OGASAWARA ISLANDS
JD1YAB

175—JD1YAB 8/31/69 (Q:158)

Chichijima is a part of the Ogasawara Islands, which were first settled by deserters from British and American whalers in the early nineteenth century. In 1867, however, a group of Japanese arrived and began to develop a large community of towns and farms that soon eclipsed the original settlers with as many as 7,000 inhabitants.

Both communities thrived on the island located 1,000 kilometers from Tokyo until 1930 when the Japanese Army arrived to fortify Chichi-jima in preparation for the war. As the US began to bomb the island, the Japanese relocated most of the civilian inhabitants, or Bonins, back to the mainland.

One of the heroes of the US attack was navy pilot George H. W. Bush, who flew his TBM "Avenger" torpedo bomber to take out the Japanese communications center. He drew anti-aircraft fire but stayed in his plane until he was able to release his payload and destroy the target. Only then did he ditch into the sea. After three hours in the water, in which Japanese boats tried to capture him only to be repelled by other US planes, he was rescued by a submarine, the USS Finback.

In late 1945, the marines took control of Chichi and demolished everything they considered of military value. A year later, 130 of the original inhabitants returned to their homes to discover a shattered infrastructure. With the help of the US Navy, they began to rebuild. SeaBees repaired the water system and set up generators, and soon industry began anew. The islanders dried and froze fish, turtles, and lobsters for export to Guam and Japan.

In 1968, the US Navy ended its 23-year term of administration and returned the island to Japan. The radio designations of the area also changed, and so six Japanese hams made this DXpedition the following August. The prefix JD1 was brand new, and for four days and nights the team operated from their tent on the beach, giving thousands of hams around the world the chance to get credit for a brand new country.

It's worth noting that there is no sign of the Vietnam War in Jerry's collection. In fact, he doesn't include contacts with any US servicemen anywhere during the primary years of the war. Jerry's family reports that there was no falloff in his ham activities during this time, and yet the volume of QSL cards does drop notably. It's hard to imagine that he was disinterested in the conflict, so the most plausible explanation is that the collection is incomplete during this period.

WOODSTOCK

MAN WALKS ON
THE MOON

ARPANET, PRECURSOR TO
MODERN INTERNET, IS BUILT

NATIONAL GUARDSMEN KILL
FOUR STUDENTS AT KENT STATE

LAND OF CALYPSO AND STEEL BAND

9Y4VV

NAZIR MOHAMED,
GASPARILLO RD.,
GASPARILLO,
TRINIDAD, W.I.
No. I SSB 7705.

176—9Y4VV 11/16/69 (I:156) SEE 039

PZ1DF

DX

YVES A. HO A CHIN

WONGLAAN 30 - P.O.BOX 523
PARAMARIBO - SURINAME S.A.

177—PZ1DF 11/16/69 (J:156) SEE 087, 178

PZ1AK

Ed D. Deira

P.O.Box : 2029
Paramaribo - Suriname S.A.

178—PZ1AK 11/23/69 (J:156)

WARKWORTH
NEW ZEALAND

ZL1PA

RADIO W2OJW WKD on 27 Nov 1969
at 0570 GMT. Ur. 14 Mc Fone/CW sigs
RST 5-5
Xmtr. Collins "S" Line   150 Watts
Ant 3 El Beam   R__ QSL TNX

Allan G. Papworth, Box 32, Warkworth, N.Z.

179—ZL1PA 11/27/69 (R:158)

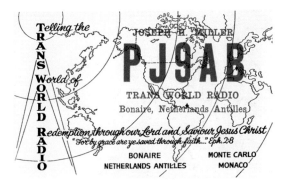

Telling the
TRANS World of WORLD RADIO

JOSEPH H. MILLER

PJ9AB

TRANS WORLD RADIO
Bonaire, Netherlands Antilles
Redemption through our Lord and Saviour Jesus Christ
"For by grace are ye saved through faith..." Eph. 2:8

BONAIRE   MONTE CARLO
NETHERLANDS ANTILLES   MONACO

180—PJ9AB 12/7/69 (H:156)

BYRD
NAVY
SUPPORTS

KC4USB

SCIENTIFIC
RESEARCH

QTH

ANTARCTICA

BC

181—KC4USB 9/26/70 (P:157)

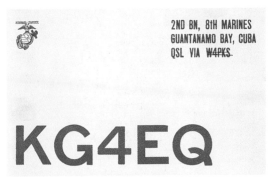

2ND BN, 8IH MARINES
GUANTANAMO BAY, CUBA
QSL VIA W4PKS

KG4EQ

182—KG4EQ 11/4/71 (G:156) SEE 064

ZF1WE

BILL EBERHARDT

19°-20'N

GRAND CAYMAN
BRITISH WEST INDIES
81°-23'W

BASED AT
PAN-CAYMAN HOUSE
ON SEVEN MILE BEACH

183—ZF1WE 7/20/72 (G:156)

BOX 200   TORTOLA   BRITISH VIRGIN ISLANDS

VP2VAP

To Radio ___W2OJW___ confirming our CW - SB - AM QSO of
_19.8.72_ at _1044_ GMT. Your _14_ MHz signals were _5-7_
Tnx for QSO Hpe to CU agn.

-------- QSL
XTMR : H·K Hanander
RCVR : Drake 2A
ANT : Morley TA 33 Tina

7x2 Vince
Vince Jardine

184—VP2VAP 8/19/72 (H:156) SEE 215

San Andres Island
"Christ our only Hope"

WA4KPH/HKØ

YL SSB'ER 8374

Confirming QSO with: ___W2OJW___

Date		GMT	MC	2-Way	RST	QSL
9.14.	19 72	2055	14.3	SSB / CW	59	PSE / TNX

73
QSL Manager
W4CPX

Ed

Rev. Edward Duncan
Box 160
San Andres Island
Colombia, S. A.

185—WA4KPH/HK0 9/14/72 (H:156)

188—HI8FMF 9/4/73 (G:156)

THE PANAMA CANAL

KZ5AL

JIM BYRD
BOX 217
GAMBOA, CANAL ZONE

189—KZ5AL 12/21/73 (H:156)

FIRST POCKET CALCULATORS

WA1QOX/Ve8
Cape Christian
Baffin Island
Canada XOA-OEO

186—WA1QDX 12/8/72 (G:156) SEE 141

BATHURST, GAMBIA, AFRICA

ZD3M

To Radio	Date	GMT	MHZ	Mode	RST
W2OJW	27 MAR 1973	1950	14	2× SSB	58/7

2 EL. QUAD **FR. MICHAEL CLEARY** 73 mike
ANTENNA **P.O. BOX 462** **TNX QSL**

187—ZD3M 3/27/73 (L:157)

REPUBLIC OF COLOMBIA

HK3 CPW
QRA: JIMMY E. KLOSE S.

HK3 CTS

QRA: MARLENE B. KLOSE S.
QTH: APARTADO 4424 BOGOTA

190—HK3CPW 12/29/73 (I:156) SEE 047

Nevis Islands, West Indies

The Birth Place of Alexander Hamilton

VP2KJ

The only Ham on the island

Radio	Date	GMT.	RST	MHz.	2 way
W2OJW	14 MAR 76	108	59	14	SSB

KEN JARVIS 73 Ken **QSL via WB2TSL**

191—VP2KJ 3/14/76 (H:156)

MARXIST PRESIDENT OF CHILE,
SALVADORE ALLENDE, IS
OVERTHROWN

180—PJ9AB

Joe Miller was a radio missionary whose card is emblazoned with the motto: "Trans World Radio. Telling the World of the Redemption through our Lord and Saviour Jesus Christ."

181—KC4USB

This contact is with the Antarctic Support Activities group of the US Navy, whose mission was to transport and support Antarctica-bound scientists and personnel. The navy launched its first polar expedition in 1838 and mapped enough of the coast to prove Antarctica was a continent.

In 1929, Admiral Richard E. Byrd flew over the South Pole from the Ross Ice Shelf in a tri-motor airplane. He returned in 1946 with the biggest Antarctic expedition ever. Nearly 5,000 men, dozens of ship, aircraft,and tractors, were put through their paces in the terrible cold to prepare them to fight the Soviet Union in polar conditions.

Today, some 3,500 scientists and support staff are based in the three US Antarctic research stations. However, cutbacks in military spending recently spelled the end of the US Navy's ability to support the bases. In 1999, the last US Navy ski-equipped LC-130 "Hercules" took off from Williams Field ending a century and a half of US Navy involvement with the frozen continent. Now the 109th Airlift Wing of the NY Air National Guard flies and maintains the fleet of "Hercs."

189—KZ5AL

In a note on the back of this card, Jim reveals that "I didn't become a novice until I was 56 years old. Looking forward to many happy years in amateur radio."

193—UA3XCA

This was Jerry's first contact with a Soviet ham, one of dozens he would make through the collapse of the USSR. While radio amateurs were allowed and even encouraged in the USSR, they were also strictly monitored, and their behavior and conversation had to be beyond reproach.

Kaluga had been on the banks of the Oka River for just over six centuries when Jerry made his way behind the Iron Curtain to visit. It had been attacked by Mongols, by revolting peasants, and by Napoleon, but Jerry was probably attracted by the role Kaluga played in the history of aerospace and engineering.

The city was the home of K. E. Tsiolkovsky (1857–1935), a self-taught high school science teacher who became the founder of cosmonautics. Well before Robert Goddard, he introduced key concepts like liquid fuel and multistage rockets and was a visionary on space travel. He wrote, "The Earth is a cradle of the human mind, but it is impossible to live in a cradle eternally."

Kaluga became a place of pilgrimage for anyone interested in the Soviet space program. In 1961, Yuri Gagarin, a ham and the first man in space, laid the cornerstone of the Aeronautics History Museum, and ever since all cosmonauts returning from space stop in to visit the city. Kaluga is still known for its scientific institutes and laboratories, and for the world's first nuclear power station.

TANGSHAN EARTHQUAKE KILLS
OVER 240,000

ATLANTIC OCEAN

Guajataca Beach

AGUADILLA

ARECIBO

El Morro Fortress

Dorada Beach

SAN JUAN

Liquillo Beach

FRANCISCO J. RODRIGUEZ
G. P. O. Box 7434
PONCE, PUERTO RICO 00731

Grapefruit Country

El Comandante
Racetrack

FAJARDO

LAS CROABAS

BARRANQUITAS

El Yunque Rain Forest

HUMACAO

Cerro De Punta
4390 Ft.

Pineapple Plantations

MAYAGUEZ

SAN GERMAN
Oldest Church

COAMO

LA PARGUERA

PONCE

Natural Springs

Phosphorescent Bay

Guayama Beach

Dewey CULEBRA IS.

PUERTO RICO

CARIBBEAN SEA KP4EGF

Isabel Segundo

VIEQUES IS.

192—KP4EGF 11/21/76 (G:156)

ZONE 16   USSR   REG 127

KALUGA

UA3XCA

DATE	GMT	TO RADIO	PS-T	MHZ	2WAY
29.5.77	H22	W2OJW	58	14	CW SSB

TRANSCEIVER   ANT  73! op SAMOFALOV VICTOR

PSE-QSL Jerry   VIA P.O. BOX 88 MOSCOW USSR

193—UA3XCA 5/29/77 (N:157)

TASMANIA
VK7AE

Confirming Two Way Communication   QSL PSE/TNX

RADIO	DATE	GMT	MHZ	MODE	RST
W2 OJW	31 Dec 77	1421	14.202	SSB	5x8

Zone 30   Wilmot Electorate   ny 73ˢ Hodie!

194—VK7AE 12/31/77 (R:158)

C6ACU
JIM DONOHUE
Simms, Long Island
BAHAMAS
←me

STATION	DATE	GMT	FREQ.	MODE	RST
W2OJW	7-16-78	1645	14331	SSB	56

195—C6ACU 7/16/78 (F:156)

GERMAN AMATEUR RADIO STATION
DK8WI   QTH-K. EK44J
DOK F Ø 7

TO RADIO: W2OJW

DATE   : 02.09.80
TIME   : 1045-55 GMT
UR RST   : 54-5 QRM
MHz   : 21.265
2-WAY   ∅SSB oCW o FM
OP: Jürgen Diehl
QTH: Eduard-Otto Str. 6
      6308 Butzbach

Thanks for the short contact Jerry

PSE QSL

73 & 55

196—DK8WI 9/2/80 (M:157)

UKRAINE
UK5MAF
CONTEST
CQ

Greetings
from
contest crew
of
coalminers

197—UK5MAF 9/9/80 (O:157) SEE 099

STAR WARS RELEASED

Ham contests are global affairs that take place several times a year. The objective is to log contact with as many other hams as possible in the allotted time, usually 24 or 48 hours.

Most contests have divisions for multioperator stations where groups work together from their club station, each operator using a different band. The ostensible point of a contest is to promote communications using a particular mode or band. Contesting is virtually a contact sport as hams from around the planet pile onto the airwaves to help teams rack up thousands of QSOs each day.

Before the fall of the USSR, the Ukraine Club Station of Coal Miners was the loudest signal coming from behind the Iron Curtain. Their founder, Stan Sychev, who arranged many of the first DXpeditions inside the USSR, even received a special Radiosport medal from the government, pronouncing him the Soviet Union's premier ham.

The Ukraine's inefficient and dangerous coal industry began in nineteenth-century Lisichansk but production has fallen sharply since the late 1980s. Exploitable coal reserves have been depleted, prices have been jacked up, and over 70 mines have been closed. Stan now lives in sunny Hayward, California and is still active in ham contests.

MOUNT ST. HELENS ERUPTS

This unspectacular card is from Thórsmörk, a very spectacular and remote natural reserve in southern Iceland nestled between the three glaciers of Eyjafjallajökull, Tindafjallajökull, and Myrdalsjökull.

Named after the Nordic thunder god, Baldvin, Thorarinsson's home is crisscrossed with ice caps and glacial rivers that make it inaccessible except to experienced guides on horseback or heavy-duty four wheel–drive vehicles. Ham radio is the only way to contact the world beyond this wild and beautiful valley full of birch forests, caves, thundering waterfalls, and the canyon of Markarfljótsgljúfur.

FOR SP-A „KS"   POLAND   ZONE 15

Adr.: Bogdan Klatka ul. Bema 43 38-404 KROSNO 4

SR8ECV

Conf our QSO

TO RADIO	DATE	UTC	MHz	2 WAY	RPRT
W2OJW	24/9 1980	17-45	21	SSB ~~CW~~	55

Pse QSL via Bureau
P.O. Box 320
00-950 Warszawa

Vy 73 es hpe cuagn
66

198—SR8ECV 9/24/80 (N:157)

GREETINGS FROM ICELAND

TF3 - Ø33

CQ ZONE 40   ITU ZONE 17

To Radio	Day	Month	Year	GMT	MHz	UR RPRT	Mode
W2OJW	25	sepT	80	12:01	21	55	☐ CW ☒ SSB

OM: JERRY

RX: ☒ YAESU FRG - 7000   I Heard your QSO with DK220
RX: ☐ NEC CQ - 110E
OTHER: _____
ANT: LONG-WIRE
PSE QSL TNX 73DE Baldi

OP: BALDVIN THORARINSSON
THORSMORK
210 GARDABAI
ICELAND

199 TF3-033 9/25/80 (M:157)

RUBIK'S CUBE CRAZE   CNN LAUNCHED

200 — UA3-170-343 (N:157)

201 — YU2CTD 9/30/80 (N:157)

202 — GM4JHG 10/14/80 (M:157)

203 — VP2MZ 10/14/80 (H:156)

204 — OH6EA 10/16/80 (N:157)

USSR KRASNODAR

UA6AZA

ALEX K. KOVGAN

205—UA6AZA 10/16/80 (N:157)

HOKKAIDO JAPAN

NO.........................

JA8IXM

CONFIRMING OUR QSO

RADIO	DATE	1ST: GMT	BAND	2WAY	RST
W2OJW	25.NOV.80	12-43	14	SSB	52

Rig _LC-201_ .... Ant _TELCONAD_ QSL ☒ PSE ☐ TNX

O P MASAAKI ITO
QTH 6 MISAWA TOMAKOMAI
HOKKAIDO 059-13 JAPAN

206—JA8IXM 11/25/80 (Q:158) SEE 276

Belgian Amateur Radio Station   Zone 14   qraCK14j

ON6BE

Felix ELSEN   Holsbeekse steenweg, 72   Kessel - Lo B 3200

DATE	GMT	STATION	QRG	MODE	RST
21.12.80	1855	W2OJW	15m	SSB	55

PSE QSL VIA U.B.A.   BOX 634   B 1000 BRUSSELS

209—ON6BE 12/29/80 (M:157)

HB9BAH

Giorgio Geiger
Via Caponelli 29
6604 Locarno
Switzerland
(canton Ticino)

DATE	TIME GMT	TO RADIO	BAND	MODE	RST
30.12.80	18.30	W2OJW	21	2X SSB	57
		OP. JERRY			

TX Trio Ts-510   ANT vert. GPA5
Pse tnx QSL via buro

73's es best dx,op. George

210—HB9BAH 12/30/80 (M:157)

206—JA8IXM

Jerry would speak with
Masaaki again eight years
later, at which point he
would receive a different
but equally banal QSL card
(see also 276).

JOHN LENNON MURDERED
IN NEW YORK CITY

DORVILLE André N 59
Lotissement de L'aiguille 97128 Goyave
Guadeloupe F.W.I

207—FG7BP 11/29/80 (H:156)

208—OH1MA/CT3 12/15/80 (L:157)

211—9K2DR 2/4/81 (O:157)

208—OH1MA/CT3

Jakko Silanto traveled from Suksela, Paimio in Finland on a DXpedition to the Madeira Islands, an archipelago about 350 miles off the coast of Morocco.

His card's design doesn't evoke the real nature of his destination but the text on the back of his card does:

"A lush flower-filled paradise with the slow pace of a more gracious age, Madeira combines European style of living with tropical appeal. We sampled the sunny island pleasures. We explored the unspoiled country and made sightseeing in

Funchal, the island's capital. We found that Christopher Columbus once lived here. Nope, the pace is faster but still gentle, gracious... just great for DX."

212—4Z4ZB 2/26/81 (N:157)

Alan Tavor, 4Z4ZB, was one of Israel's leading hams (yes, that term is quite kosher there). He lived on the Shoresh Moshav, a remote agricultural cooperative.

On August 1, 1983, with his antenna set at 45 degrees over Tel Aviv, Alan managed to make contact with the space shuttle Challenger as it flew a couple of hundred miles overhead. For a few minutes, he chatted with astronaut ham, Dr. Tony England, W0ORE, who reported Israel looked great from space before the signal slowly faded away.

In 1985, Alan was instrumental in establishing Israel's Silent Key Forest, a memorial to hams around the world who have passed away. At least once a year, amateurs gather amidst the thousands of trees planted in tribute to their silent comrades. They also hold gatherings and field days there on the Hadid ridge between Tel Aviv and Jerusalem.

Sadly, Alan's name joined those in the forest when his key was silenced by a heart attack at age 52.

IBM INTRODUCES FIRST
PERSONAL COMPUTER

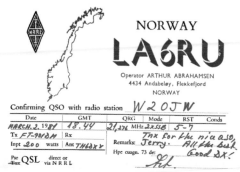

NORWAY
LA6RU
Operator ARTHUR ABRAHAMSEN
4434 Andabeløy, Flekkefjord
NORWAY

Confirming QSO with radio station   W 2 0 J W

Date	GMT	QRG	Mode	RST	Conds
MARCH. 2. 1981	18.44	21,274 MHz 2x55B	5-7		

Tx FT-901DM Rx
Inpt 200 watts Ant TH6DXX
Remarks: Tnx for the nice QSO,
Jerry. All the best
Hpe cuagn. 73 de: Good DX!

Pse QSL direct or
Tnx   via N R R L

213 LA6RU 3/2/81 (M157)

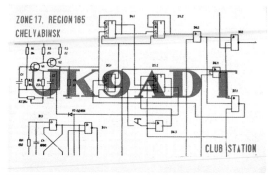

ZONE 17, REGION 165
CHELYABINSK

UK9ADT

CLUB STATION

214 UK9ADT 3/6/81 (O:157)

VP2VIA

KØPCG 1981 DXPEDITION TO TORTOLA, B.V.I.

215—VP2VIA 3/25/81 (H:156)

GERMAN DEMOCRATIC REPUBLIC
VEB Gaskombinat Schwarze Pumpe
Y 53 ZF
We work up brown-coal into: Briquettes; coke;
sewergas and produce steam; electricity and thermal energy.

216—Y53ZF 6//11/81 (N:157)

To Radio: W 2- O. J. W.
Mrs. Yursy

P.A.3-A.K.D
GIJS VAN SON
Tienhont 7
5301 VM Zaltbommel, Holland

Transcvr.: TS 180 S
            H.W. 100
Ant.:   Zep - Mini Quad
Opr.:   Gijs

QSO nr	Day	Month	Year	GMT	MHZ	Mode	RST	Remarks
168	25	8	81	1705	21=	5.9	SSB	73 Jerry

Pse - Tnx - QSL via P.O.Box 400, Rotterdam, Holland R30

217—PA3AKD 8/25/81 (M:157)

214—UK9ADT

Chelyabinsk has the dubious distinction of being named the most polluted spot on earth.

Beginning in the early 1950s, the Mayak weapons plant dumped radioactive waste in the river that provided water for the area. Instead of evacuating or cleaning up the area, the authorities strung barbed wire along the river banks. Then the radioactive containment unit malfunctioned and blew up. Finally, when a drought dried up the local lake in 1967, radioactive dust was blown across 25,000 square kilometers. In all, a half million people received five million curies of radiation.

Despite this epic disaster, Jerry probably wouldn't have found Chelyabinsk on any map. The city of over a million is in the South Urals at the geographical center of Russia, but, as far as the Soviet authorities were concerned, the site didn't officially exist. For 45 years, Chelyabinsk was closed to all foreigners.

Except those with ham radios.

ASSASSINATION ATTEMPT ON
RONALD REAGAN

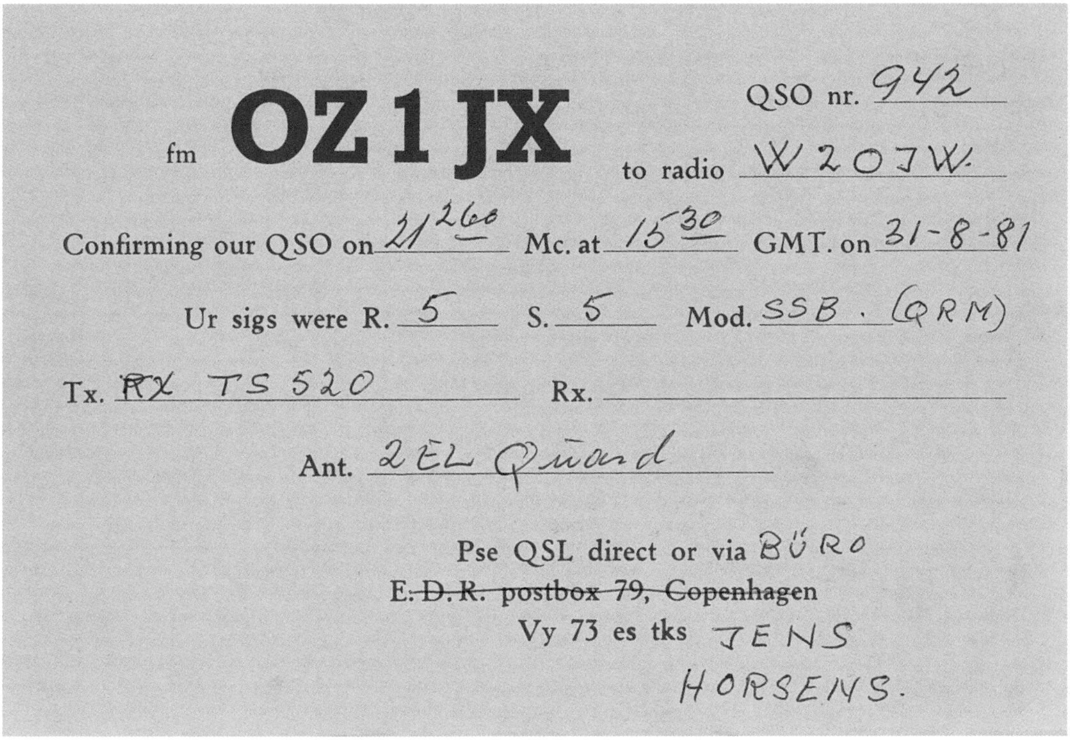

fm **OZ 1 JX**

QSO nr. *942*

to radio *W 2 O J W.*

Confirming our QSO on *21 260* Mc. at *15 30* GMT. on *31-8-81*

Ur sigs were R. *5* S. *5* Mod. *SSB . (QRM)*

Tx. *RX TS 520* Rx. _____

Ant. *2 EL Quard*

Pse QSL direct or via *BÜRO*

~~E. D. R. postbox 79, Copenhagen~~

Vy 73 es tks *JENS*

HORSENS.

218—OZ1JX 8/31/81 (N:157)

215—VP2VIA

Nick Critelli and his son traveled from Des Moines, Iowa to Tortola in the British Virgin Islands for a pleasant four-day DXpedition. While enjoying the frangipani, mangoes, and balmy trade winds, they managed to provide a new country for the 2,000 hams they contacted.

216—Y53ZF

This QSO was a glimpse behind the Iron Curtain. Helmut Hansch of Hoyers- werda in East Germany provided this lovely pic- ture of the VEB Gaskombinat Schwarze Pumpe, which proudly turns brown coal into briquettes and sewer gas, and produces steam electricity and thermal energy. A place probably best visited by radio.

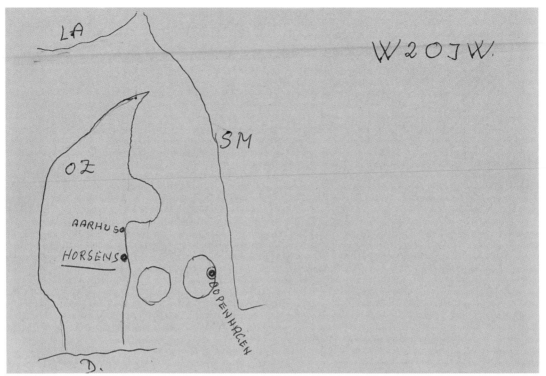

LA

W2OJW.

SM

OZ

AARHUS•

HORSENS•

COPENHAGEN

D.

218—OZ1JX (BACK)

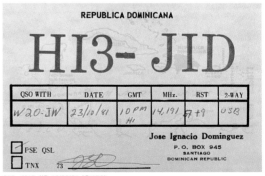

REPUBLICA DOMINICANA

HI3- JID

QSO WITH	DATE	GMT	MHz.	RST	2-WAY
W2O-JW	23/10/81	10 PM HI	14,191	57 +9	USB

☑ PSE QSL

☐ TNX   73

Jose Ignacio Dominguez
P.O. BOX 945
SANTIAGO
DOMINICAN REPUBLIC

219—H13-JID 10/23/81 (G:156)

AIDS VIRUS IDENTIFIED

CALL SIGNS

Every ham and his station have a unique call sign, the alphanumeric sequence that is usually the most prominent thing on the QSL card. It identifies the user and his location to other hams and to the government organization overseeing the airwaves. When he was a boy in Kansas, Jerry's first call sign was W9DOG but, like his car's license plate, it changed after he moved to New Jersey, and he was known thereafter as W2OJW.

Until recently (when vanity licenses were finally allowed), a ham had no choice as to the numbers and letters assigned to his station. Each call is composed of a letter and number prefix, which is specific to his country, and a three-letter suffix that is unique to the particular ham. Jerry's prefix was W2 for New York and New Jersey, and his suffix were the letters O, J, and W.

The International Telecommunications Union (ITU) assigns a range of call signs to each country that has amateur radio status, and there's no obvious link between the country name and its assigned prefix. The prefix generally consists of one or two letters and a number, like MA8 for the Isle of Guernsey or W8 for Michigan, Ohio, and West Virginia. Some countries have prefixes that begin with a number followed by a letter. For example, 7S is Sweden and 7X is Algeria. The two countries are far apart on the map but not in the prefix alphabet.

When he's on the air in his own ham shack, a ham's call sign is his identity, far more so than his legal name. He must announce the sign at least once every ten minutes during a contact and again when he signs off. It's not unusual for a ham to emblazon his call sign on his license plates and clothing. Occasionally, special call signs that are easily recognizable will be allocated for special events. For instance, DXpeditions are frequently given a special call sign assigned just for the duration of the trip.

If a ham travels to another region, he is working "portable" and would mention that in his call. If Jerry went back to Kansas (W0) for a visit and got on the air, he would identify himself with a special suffix as W2OJW/W0. In most parts of the world, he would have used a portable prefix, so in the hugely unlikely event that he left his basement in Hackensack and got on the air in Chile (3G) he would have called himself 3G portable W2OJW or 3G/W2OJW.

FIG. 24–26
Station call letters
from QSL cards
(details)

VE: Vancouver,
British Columbia,
Canada

JA: Kanazawa, Japan

W0: Knoxville, Iowa,
USA

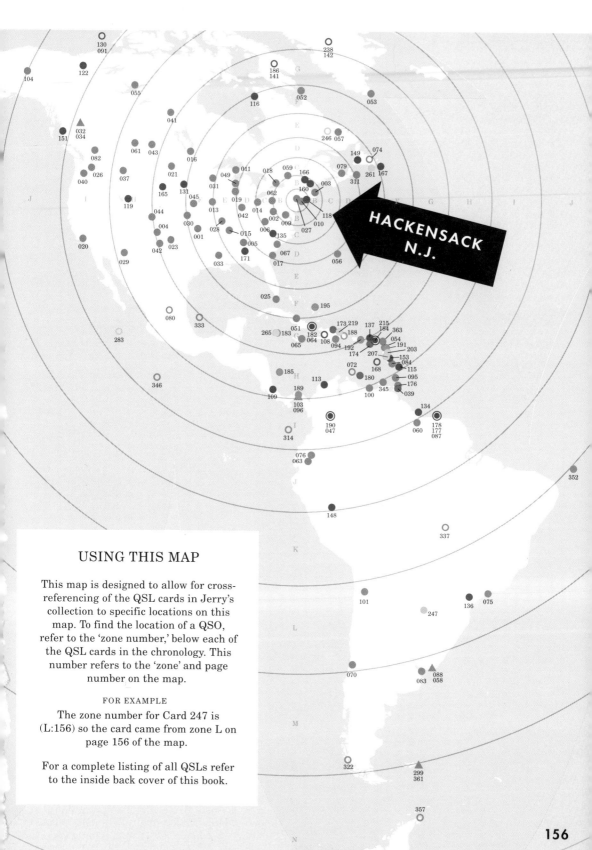

HACKENSACK N.J.

USING THIS MAP

This map is designed to allow for cross-referencing of the QSL cards in Jerry's collection to specific locations on this map. To find the location of a QSO, refer to the 'zone number,' below each of the QSL cards in the chronology. This number refers to the 'zone' and page number on the map.

FOR EXAMPLE

The zone number for Card 247 is (L:156) so the card came from zone L on page 156 of the map.

For a complete listing of all QSLs refer to the inside back cover of this book.

W2OJW

AND W9DOG

RADIO ACTIVITY

BY DECADE

(CONFIRMED BY QSL)

OPERATOR:

JERRY POWELL

HACKENSACK, NEW JERSEY
USA

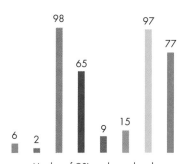

98

97

77

65

15

6   2   9

Number of QSL cards per decade

- ● 1920 *thru* 1929
- ● 1930 *thru* 1939
- ● 1940 *thru* 1949
- ● 1950 *thru* 1959
- ● 1960 *thru* 1969
- ● 1970 *thru* 1979
- ○ 1980 *thru* 1989
- ● 1990 *thru* 1999

▲   More that one contact with the
    same location in the same
    decade

◉   More than one contact with the
    same location in a different
    decade(s)

○   Location unknown

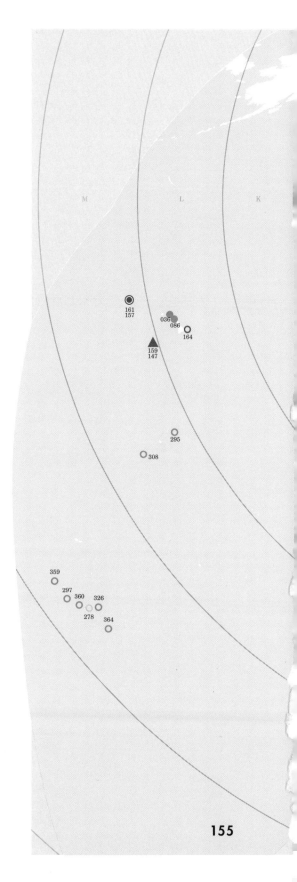

hello

world

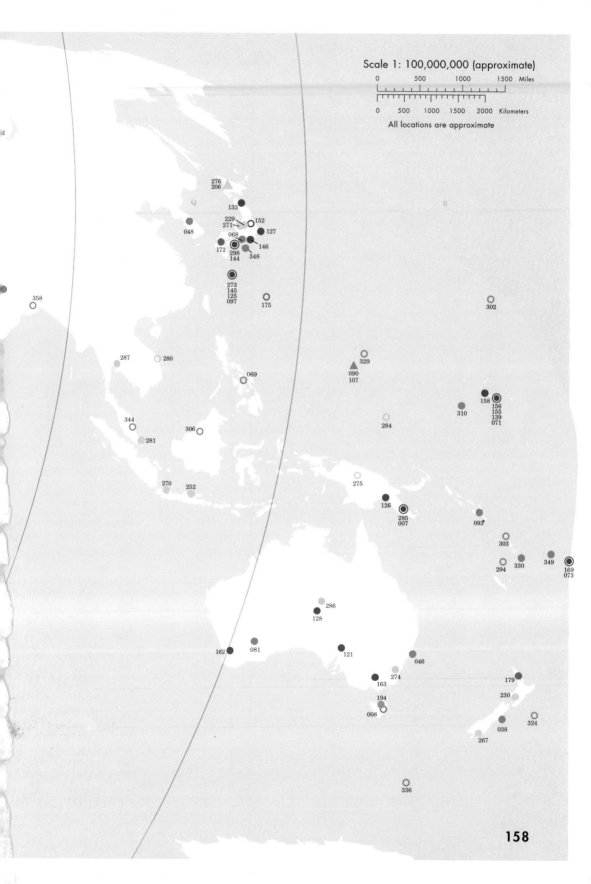

Scale 1: 100,000,000 (approximate)

0   500   1000   1500   Miles

0   500   1000   1500   2000   Kilometers

All locations are approximate

276
206

133

Q   R

229
271   152
048   127
         068
172   146
   298 348
   144

273
145
125
097   175   302

358

287   280

                069

                    329
                  090
                  107

                                   158 156
                                        155
                              310   139
                                        071

344   284

306
281

270
252

                    275

                126
                285
                007   093

                              303

                          294 330 349 169
                                        073

              286
          128

162   081
              121
                    046

              163 274   179
              194   230
              008   324

                              038
                          267

                    336

158

PUBLIC SERVICE

At the heart of all ham activities—the codes, the competitions, the DXpeditions, the self-imposed tests and exercises—lies the radio amateur's commitment to public service. While the hobby is great fun, it is licensed and encouraged in order to maintain a self-supporting and dependable communications infrastructure in case of emergency.

Across the ham community, there is a universal commitment to helping out, and many hams have great stories of when they were able to pass on the word and lend a hand. Time and again, hams have saved the lives of stranded sailors by relaying news of their plight to the Coast Guard. They have guided emergency services to people left homeless by tornadoes or floods and provided updates on their situations to worried relatives far away. And in times of national emergency like September 11, 2001 in New York City (see introduction), amateur radio has been an essential link in the most vital communications systems.

During natural disasters, hams connect people to people who can save their lives. When lines are down and power is out, they move in to the effected areas and set up temporary hamshacks and "traffic nets" specifically designed to hand off messages quickly and efficiently. They are often the only form of communication that can reach federal, emergency, and law enforcement authorities, and relay messages to anxious loved ones, sometimes on the other side of the world. They help to direct shipments of medical supplies, coordinate sandbagging efforts, and guide assistance to sinking ships. It's not unusual for volunteer hams to remain on site until regular communications are reestablished, giving up days and weeks of their time.

FIG. 27
Advertisement
Hallicrafters,
1952.

CIVIL DEFENSE

The Radio Amateur Civil Emergency Service (RACES) was established in 1952 so that amateurs could provide a communications network in case of a serious national emergency. Connections were made between hams and local emergency services and civil defense authorities, a system that still operates today under the auspices of the Federal Emergency Management Agency (FEMA). Registered hams can conduct drills on certain frequencies, overriding all other traffic in the area.

МОСКВА '80

220—UB5BAZ 11/9/81 (N:157)

LUXEMBOURG

LX1 SR /P /M

OP: Serge RABINGER

QTN: 7, rue Nurkes
Beringen / Mersch

LUXEMBOURG

TO RADIO W2 OJW

Confirming our 2-way CW·FM·AM·SSB QSO

at 19.45 GMT/MEZ Date NOV. 16.81

on 21 Mc. R-S-S-5-7 M

QRM_____ QRN_____ QSB_____

Rig. TS-520 S_____

Ant. Delen 34 steel_____

Wx._____

Remarks Tnx for th QSO

Good Luck as vy 73/88

Pse/tnx QSL via club or direct

221—LX1SR 11/16/81 (M:157)

ITALY AMATEUR RADIO STATION - ZONE 15

I4UJB

GIANCARLO SPINELLI
Via Colombara, 449 S. ANDREA IN B. - 47023 CESENA ITALY

Radio	Date	GMT	MHZ	RST	MODE	RTX-ANT
W2 OJW	4.12.81	1736	21	55	SSB	FT505
						TA33

73'   PSE - QSL - ~~TNX~~

222—I4UJB 12/4/81 (M:157)

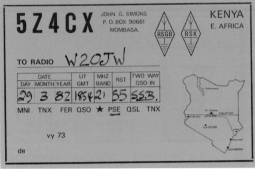

5Z4CX

JOHN. G. SIMONS
P. O. BOX 90661
MOMBASA.

RSGB RSK

KENYA
E. AFRICA

TO RADIO W2OJW

DATE DAY MONTH YEAR	UT GMT	MHZ BAND	RST	TWO WAY QSO IN
29 3 82	1854	21	55	S.S.B.

MNI TNX FER QSO ★ PSE QSL TNX

vy 73

de

225—5Z4CX 3/29/82 (O:157)

BALEARIC ISLANDS

URE

EA6 FC

To Radio W2 OJW   Confirming our QSO:

DATE	GMT	MHZ	MODE	RST
30/3/82	1920	21	2 x SSB	5/8

PSE TNX QSL
TNX FOR QSO
73's

DELEGACION URE
P. O Box, 20
FELANITX (Balearic Is.)

226—EA6FC 3/30/82 (M:157)

JCC #0914

JA0 WRF

NAGANO JAPAN

Ryuji Nakayama
1378-12, Toyohira, Chino City,
Nagano 391-02 Japan

Nagano pref.
Chino Tokyo
Osaka
Mt. Yatsu Mt. Fuji
Lake Suwa

229—JA0WRF 8/6/82 (Q:158)

Kia Ora from # ZL2AHR

New Zealand

GRAHAM HAWTREE.
26 STEWART ST.,
WANGANUI, N.Z.

WANGANUI

To RADIO W2OJW/JERRY

PH/CW QSO on 142.78

TIME 0816 aton 29-8-1982

R 5 S 1 T

EQUIP TS 520 SE

ANT THS Beam

PSE/TNX QSL   73's Graham

J. W. Lee Print, 48 Tinirau St. Wanganui, N.Z.

BRANCH 48

230—ZL2AHR 9/29/82 (R:158)

ARGENTINA INVADES FALKLAND
ISLANDS

FRANCE
F6FTB
ex FB8XV

Zone : 14
Dpt : 91
Loc : Bi22c

2-WAY	QSO - QSL WITH	DATE	GMT	MHz	RST	QSL
SSB	W2OJW	JAN 05th 82	18 53	21268	59	PSE TNX

Christian GONDARD
Apt. 52
69, rue de Paris
F 91400 ORSAY

Thanks Jerry for mke œ80 73, *Chris*
Good luck and DX!

223—F6FTB 1/5/82 (M:157)

Z 21Gi FORMERLY
ZEIGI ZIMBABWE

224—ZEIGI 2/3/82 (O:157) SEE 367

CANARY ISLANDS
ZONE 33
EA 8 QY

To Radio	W 2 OJW			Confirming our QSO:
DATE	GMT	MHZ	RST	MODE - 2 WAY
J. J. 82	18.00	21	J/5	CW - RTTY / SSB - FM

KENWOOD
TS - 520

DIPOLO
AS - 33

PSE TNX QSL
TNX FOR QSO
73's & DX's

OCTAVIO GUERRA MUÑOZ
Fernando Guanarteme, 32.- Aptdo. 2?
LAS PALMAS DE GRAN CANARIA
Telf.: 26 20 80
Islas Canarias

op: JERRX

227—EA8QY 5/5/82 (L:157)

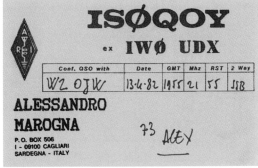

ISØQOY
ex IWØ UDX

Conf. QSO with	Date	GMT	Mhz	RST	2 Way
W2 OJW	13-4-82	1955	21	55	SSB

ALESSANDRO
MAROGNA
P. O. BOX 506
I - 09100 CAGLIARI
SARDEGNA - ITALY

73 ALEX

228—IS0QOY 6/13/82 (M:157)

ST. VALENTIN
Protektor of our village

OE 3 HKA
AUSTRIA AMATEUR RADIO STATION
Op:
HELMUT KÖNIG
QTH:
HERZOGRAD 28
A-4300 ST.VALENTIN
QRA HI 63j

231—OE3HKA 9/28/82 (R:158)

USSR
Ukraine Lvov
UB5QS
ex: rb5bfe

232—UB5QS 10/9/82 (N:157)

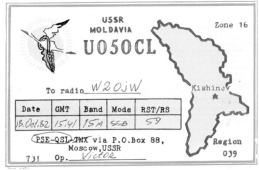

USSR
MOLDAVIA
UO50CL
Zone 16

To radio W2OjW

Date	GMT	Band	Mode	RST/RS
18.Oct.82	15,41	15M	SSB	59

PSE-QSL-TNX via P.O.Box 88,
Moscow,USSR
731 Op. Victor

Kishinev
Region 039

233—U050CL 10/18/82 (N:157)

Antrim is the home of one of Northern Ireland's greatest distilleries but GI4NRB's conversation was probably not about Bushmill's whiskey. The IRA had been making headlines around the world for the past year, ever since their leader, Bobby Sands had begun his hunger strike in Maze Prison.

By the time the strike was called off in October of 1981, Sands and nine others were dead. On July 20, 1982, the IRA exploded two bombs in Hyde Park in London, killing eight British soldiers. Three months later, on the day of Jerry's call, the first elections were held to the

new 78-seat Northern Ireland Assembly. Sinn Féin, while not recognizing Northern Ireland as a political entity, ran and won five seats. This emergence of the IRA as a political force ushered in a new era in Northern Irish history. Jerry was there.

GI4NRB

RSGB

To A.R.S. W2OJW

Confirming Our QSO of,

Date	GMT	MHz
20-10-82	1730	21

Mode	RST
J3E	58-

Pse Tnx QSL   Via RSGB ~~Direct~~

W. J. (Bill) WATSON, 6 CROMWELL'S HIGHWAY, LISBURN, Co. ANTRIM N.I.

234—GI4NRB 10/20/82 (M:157)

SPIELBERG'S *E.T.* OPENS

235—G4LGW

The next day, Jerry got the
British point of view on the
changes in Northern
Ireland.

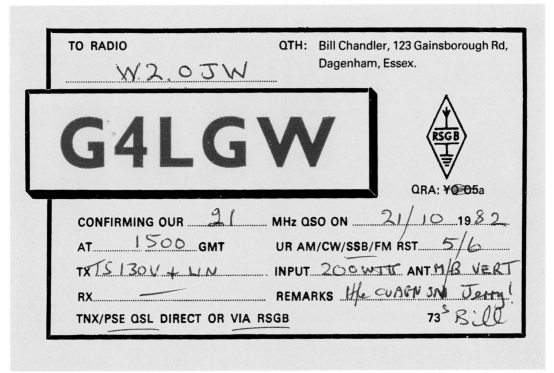

TO RADIO   QTH: Bill Chandler, 123 Gainsborough Rd,
Dagenham, Essex.

W2OJW

G4LGW

RSGB

QRA: YO 05a

CONFIRMING OUR ___21___ MHz QSO ON ___21/10___ 19__82__

AT ___1500___ GMT   UR AM/CW/SSB/FM RST ___5/6___

TX __TS 130V + WN__ . INPUT __200 WTT__ ANT __M/B VERT__

RX _____ REMARKS __tfe CUAGN SN Jerry!__

TNX/PSE QSL DIRECT OR VIA RSGB   73s Bill

235—G4LGW 10/21/82 (M:157)

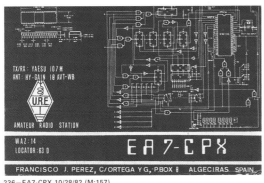

TX/RX : YAESU 107M
ANT : HY-GAIN 18 AVT-WB

URE

AMATEUR RADIO STATION

WAZ: 14
LOCATOR: 63 D

EA7-CPX

FRANCISCO J. PEREZ, C/ORTEGA Y G., P.BOX 8   ALGECIRAS   SPAIN

236—EA7-CPX 10/28/82 (M:157)

ARS A22FY/H5ADW   AFRICA

TO RADIO W5OJW _____ **CONFIRMING OUR QSO OF**

DATE	UTC	BAND	RST	MODE	TX	KENWOOD TS-130S
15 DEC 82	1843	21MHz	5X9	2X SSB	RX	
					ANT	INVERTED "V"

PSE QSL DIRECT:

A22FY/H5ADW

P.O. Box 600

MAFIKENG, BOPHUTHATSWANA

— PSE QSL X TNX

BEST 73'S,
S T A N
A22FY
H5ADW

237 — A22FY/H5ADW 12/15/82 (O:157)

Strangely enough, Mafikeng, this small town in north central South Africa, is indirectly responsible for the worldwide spread of the ham radio bug.

In 1899, Mafikeng was the administrative capital of the British Protectorate of Bechuanaland, now Botswana. The British garrison was under siege by thousands of Boers and thoroughly outmanned by the enemy. The British general-in-charge, Robert Stephenson Baden-Powell, was extremely resourceful. He devised a series of clever tricks and ruses to hold off the Boer and, by training a group of boys to perform many of the noncombatant roles, freed up all the men to fight the battle. The boys ran messages and stood watch. After 217 days, British relief forces arrived and ended the siege.

That group of boys continued to grow and develop after the siege battle and eventually grew to 30 million worldwide, the modern Boy Scouts. Mafikeng is still recognized as the cradle of scouting, and the fort has become a monument that attracts tourists from all over.

The Boy Scouts movement is the place many people first encountered amateur radio; and the hobby is a natural fit. It's wholesome, intellectually challenging, and constructive, and helps to forge bonds with people from many lands. Many hams volunteer to share their hobby with local troops, and thousands of 11- to 14-year-olds are still awarded Radio Merit Badges.

OX3AE

238—OX3AE 12/15/82 (H:156)

5H3MI

OP: Christer
SM5NDM

Lake Victoria
Mwanza
Muhange Kibondo
KEZA
Arusha
Kifura
Kigoma
Tabora
Dodoma
Dar es Salaam
TANZANIA

NOMIRA the nordic missionary radio amateurs

239—5H3MI 2/24/83 (O:157)

73

UK2AAW

240—UK2AAW 7/9/83 (N:157)

Sweden SM7LPY

241—SM7LPY 9/29/83 (N:157)

EUROPE   SICILY ISLAND   ZONE 15

IT9-HLR

CONFIRMING QSO   Op. SALVO

DAY	MONTH	YEAR	GMT	MHz	STATION	RST	TWO WAY	QSL
20	02	84	16.47	21	W2OJW	5/4	SSB	TKS PSE

73 TKS QSO

P. O. Box 11
96100 SIRACUSA ITALY

242—IT9HLR 2/20/84 (N:157)

HA 6 KNV

HUNGARY
Europe   QTH: SZÉCSENY

WPX ZONE 15

TO RADIO	DATE	UT	MHz	RST	2 WAY	INPUT
W203W	26. III. 84.	17.02	21	59	SSB	100 W / ANT / 3 ele

TNX PSE QSL VIA Sori Jerry, very much VY 73 ES BEST DX!
MRASZ QSL BUREAU agn. but thanks
H-1368 BUDAPEST   for n/se QSO.   John
P. O. BOX 214   Please send your QSL.

243—HA6KNV 3/26/84 (N:157)

ВЛАДИМИР   — SOVIET UNION —

UA3WG

op. Vladimir Petrovichev

COLL	DATE	GMT	MC	2-WAY	RST/M
W2Ojw	14.05.84	16 05	21	SSB	58

QTH - VLADIMIR   PSE - QSL - TNH
Zone-16 Region-119   P.O. Box 88 Moscow - USSR

245—UA3WG 5/14/84 (N:157)

CANADA

VO2AM

Craig McLoughlin
809 Lakeside Drive
Labrador City, Newfoundland
A2V 1C2

246—VO2AM 5/17/84 (E:156)

239—5H3MI

A Swedish missionary posted in Tanzania.

240—UK2AAW

The Morse code next to the handshake spells out "73" for "best regards."

244—YO6XA

This card is from Alois Fleischman (YO6XA) in Romania.

244—YO6XA 4/18/84 (N:157)

OWEN GARRIOTT, W5LFL, BECOMES THE FIRST HAM TO OPERATE IN SPACE ON BOARD A SPACE SHUTTLE

US EMBASSY IN BEIRUT BOMBED

247—ZP5RG

While most hams operate out of their shacks or in-home stations, restrictions on antennas, interference from power lines, phones, computers, and TVs can limit indoor operation. Many amateurs have special equipment they can take along and quickly set up anywhere outdoors.

A compact HF or VHF transceiver, a small power source like a lead acid battery or a solar panel, and a telescoping antenna can put one in contact with the world from any remote hilltop. Some hams carry a sling shot with a fishing reel attached: they can aim at the tallest branches of a tree and fire their antenna wire up to snag the best point for reception. Mobile equipment can be operated in cars, boats, and trains; or even, like Z55RG, an American diplomat in Uruguay, does on mule-back.

248—PY1-VOY/PY0T

The members of the CWRJ DXpedition go to great lengths to make it clear that they are interested only in CW or Morse code communications.

Nonetheless, this QSL card records that this contact with Jerry was SSB, a single-side band voice communication.

EL SALVADOR ELECTS MODERATE JOSÉ NAPOLEÓN DUARTE TO PRESIDENCY

INDIRA GANDHI ASSASSINATED BY TWO SIKH BODYGUARDS

ASUNCION ZP5RG PARAGUAY

ONE HORSEPOWER MOBILE
EX-CPIDN-PT2ZAB- 8R1R

MALCOLM CHRIS JENSEN
331 SAN JOSE ASUNCION-PARAGUAY

247—ZP5RG 9/13/84 (L:156)

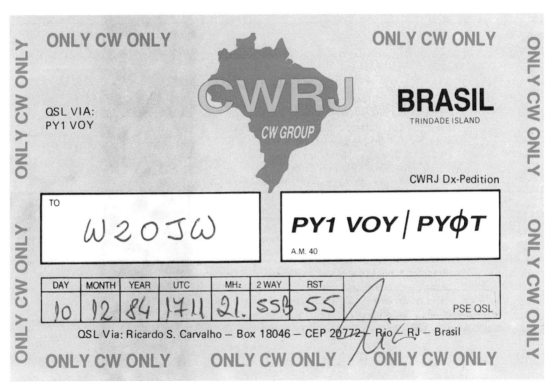

ONLY CW ONLY

ONLY CW ONLY

QSL VIA:
PY1 VOY

CWRJ
CW GROUP

BRASIL
TRINDADE ISLAND

CWRJ Dx-Pedition

TO							
W2OJW				**PY1 VOY / PYØT** A.M. 40			

DAY	MONTH	YEAR	UTC	MHz	2 WAY	RST	
10	12	84	1711	21.	SSB	55	PSE QSL

QSL Via: Ricardo S. Carvalho — Box 18046 — CEP 20772 — Rio — RJ — Brasil

ONLY CW ONLY   ONLY CW ONLY   ONLY CW ONLY

248—PY1-VOY/PY0 12/10/84 (M:156)

1ЫЙ ЧЕМПИОНАТ ЕВРОПЫ ПО РАДИОТЕЛЕГРАФИИ

UA9-140-990

249—UA9-140-990 2/26/85 (O:157)

249—UA9-140-990

Igor was transmitting from Solikamsk, which produces the salt of the Earth: potassium and potassium-magnesium, chloride, sodium, and other minerals have been mined here since the 1430s. The town's name means "the salt of the river Kamsk," and its coat of arms features a bucket used for hauling brine. Despite loads of landmark seventeenth-century architecture, Solikamsk's environment is dangerously polluted and very unsafe for its 100,000 residents, most of whom work in the local chemical industry.

250—UA3-121-3160 3/26/85 (N:157)

FAMINE IN ETHIOPIA   WRECK OF THE TITANIC LOCATED

252—YB3CEV

Yan Bambang Susanto lives in Surabaya: Indonesia's second largest city. He became a ham in 1980 and had only been DXing for a couple of years when he talked to W2OJW. He still recalls his long contact with Jerry. Despite the less than ideal reception, and the great differences in their ages and backgrounds, they had a rich conversation. Yan recalls,

"When I heard his voice, I certainly know (sic) that he is *really* an old man."

Yan has gone on to receive hundreds of awards in his career as a DXer including WAS (Worked all [United] States).

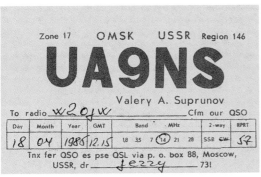

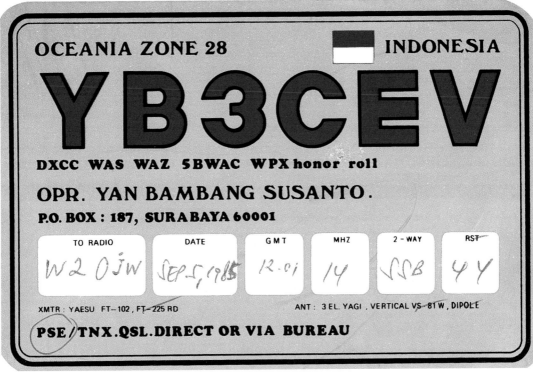

Max de Henseler, former Secretary of the United Nations Group of Experts on Geographical Names (UNGEGN), came to be known as "Mr. UN Amateur Radio" for his contributions to the hobby. He and Jerry met at one of the meetings of the Quarter Century Wireless Association, after Jerry became the president of his local chapter. While Jerry included this card in his collection, it is a confirmation not of a contact over the radio but in person, a so-called "eyeball QSO."

253—HB9RS/W2 10/6/85 (M:157)

REAGAN AND GORBACHEV MEET AT SUMMIT

PLACES

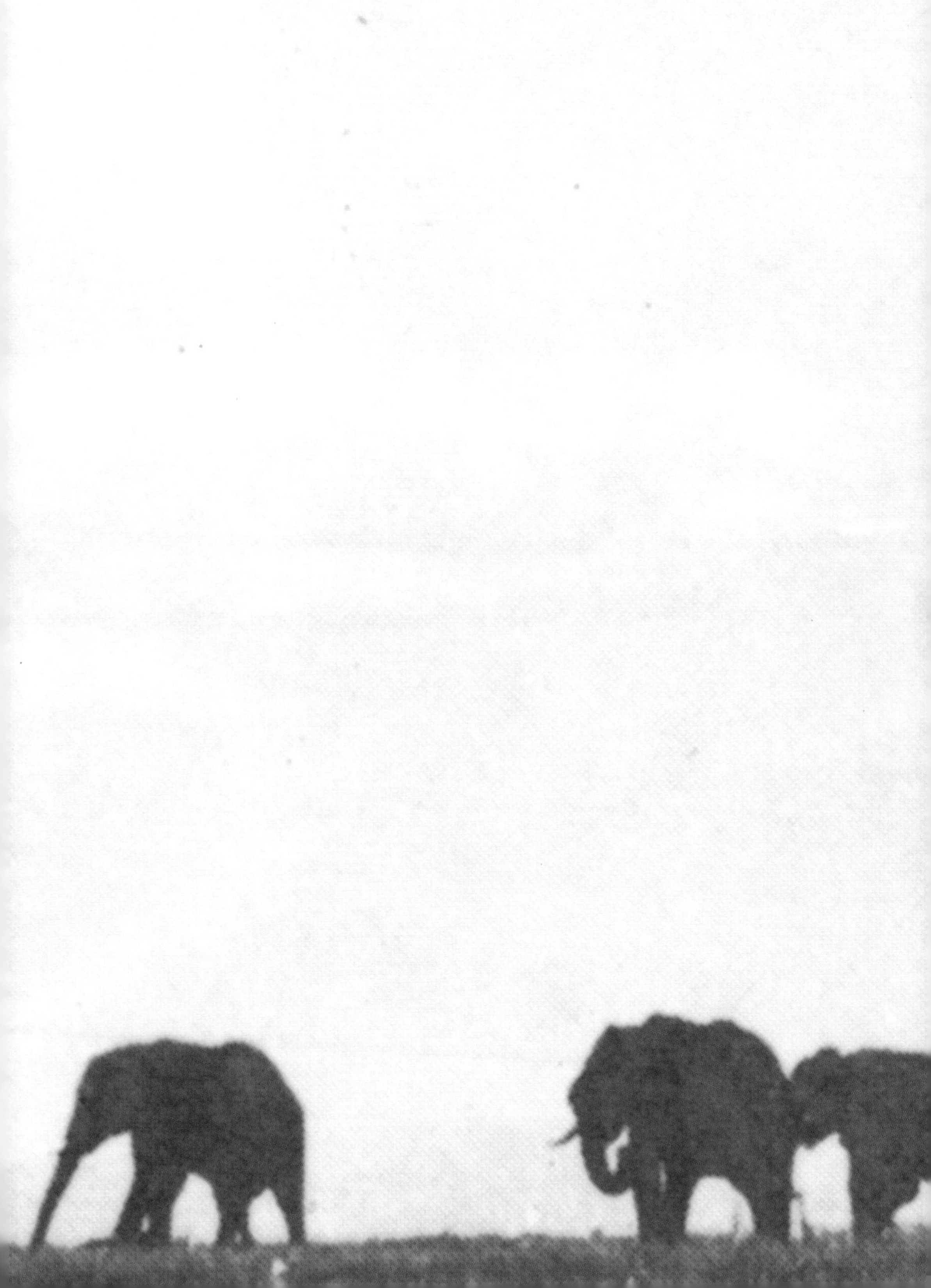

255—OH2BEN/C56

The Gambia is the smallest and westernmost nation in Africa and a hard one to score for most DXers. Tomi Laakkonen traveled there from his home in Vantaa, Finland for this DXpedition in the summer of 1985. With the help of two local hams, he set up his tri-band vertical antenna, his Yaesu FT 757GX, and his Kenwood AT230 in the Hotel Kombo Beach. He made 4,000 contacts from the beach and, once he got home to Finland, sent each of them one of these cards to prove they had made contact with a new country.

257—UB5TCS

Jerry's second visit to the Ukraine this week. The picture on this card shows the mighty walls of one of the country's oldest towns, walls that seem to grow right out of the steep stony banks of the Smotrich River. The town has a rich architectural history, full of towers (built by competing trade guilds), minarets, and church steeples that lure hundreds of thousands of tourists each year.

259—S83CA

This card features the symbol of Polski Zwiazek Krotkofalowcow, the Polish radio club, founded in 1930 and representing hams in the International Amateur Radio Union ever since.

260—4U1ITU

Carl was transmitting from the ITU headquarters in Geneva, Switzerland. The International Telecommunications Union is the specialized UN agency for telecommunications. At the time, it boasted 160 members.

261—FP/KA1CRP

Dave Landry set up this typical small-scale DXpedition alone after a fellow ham backed out at the last minute. He flew to Halifax, waited for the fog to burn off, then hopped across to the cold wet rocks of Saint Pierre and Miquelon. These misty islands, just south of Newfoundland, are the last vestiges of the once great possessions of France in North America. In fact, Dave reports that getting visas from France was the most arduous part of his trip.

Once the expedition was launched, Dave enjoyed the fine hotels and restaurants of "fp." In six days, he made 4,000 contacts with people from around the world, then traveled home and sent them all QSL cards like this one.

Dave became a ham in the Coast Guard in 1979. He is an avid DXer, loving the chase of tracking down distant stations; 95% of his contacts are with people in foreign countries. He also enjoys collecting QSL cards, saying, "You can say you talked to anybody but as they used to say in an old commercial, 'where's the beef?' They're the proof the contact actually took place."

263—UK1NAD

Karelia shuttled back and forth from Finland to Sweden to Russia several times in its long history as a front line between East and West. Despite its integration into the USSR during World War II and the virtual eradication of its distinct culture, the Iron Curtain around Karelia was fairly porous. At this time of *glasnost*, Karelia was an important point for cross-border trade and cultural exchange.

265—ZF2KZ

This was another Finnish DXpedition; Jan Hubach and his friend Arja Nyman set up a beacon on Grand Cayman Island and began transmitting to the world. When they finished their work, they donated their gear to appreciative local hams.

268—UQ2GJN

As Gorbachev's reforms took hold, Jerry made more and more contacts with Soviet hams, from Oskar in Latvia to Rein Kolk in Estonia to Serge in Rajchihinsk.

276—JA8IXM

This was Jerry's second QSL from Masaaki Ito (see also 206). Clearly he was very proud of his IC-780 transceiver.

CYPRUS 1960 - 1985

25 YEARS

5B25OK

PHEDIAS S. SPANIAS
P. O. BOX 9087
NICOSIA - CYPRUS

254—5B25OK 10/17/85 (N:157)

OH2BEN/C56
THE REPUBLIC OF THE GAMBIA
AFRICA, ZONE 35

255—OH2BEN/C56 11/7/85 (L:157)

- OHØNJ -

ALAND ISLANDS 73 de

TO	W2OJW	
DATE		GMT
860111		1357
RST		② S S B
S8		2 × C W
		2 × F M
		2 × RTTY

1,8 3,5 7 ⑭ 21 28 144
COUNTY·007·JOMALA
QTH L. JU70C
CQ ZONE15, ITU ZONE18
ISSB 8636, 5BDXCC 501

EINAR LINDHOLM
BOX 88
SF-22210 GÖLBY
FINLAND

258—OHØNJ 11/1/86 (N:157)

S83CA

TRANSKEI

259—S83CA 11/6/86 (O:157)

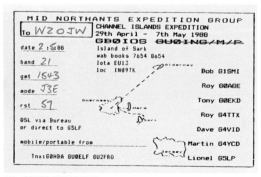

OK2BJR
C Z E C H O S L O V A K I A

MILOŠ BREGIN
783 46 TĚŠETICE 73
OKRES OLOMOUC

262—OK2BJR 9/3/87 (N:157)

KARELIA USSR

UK1NAD

EX UN1KAI, U1NV

RADIOCLUB „LADOGA"

ZONE 16 EUROPE REG 088
SORTAVALA

263—UK1NAD 9/29/87 (N:157)

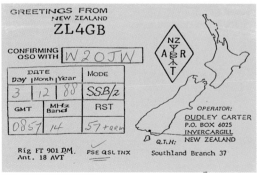

MID NORTHANTS EXPEDITION GROUP
CHANNEL ISLANDS EXPEDITION
29th April - 7th May 1988

To W2OJW

GB0IOS 8U0ING/M/P.
Island of Sark
wab books 7654 8654
Iota EU13
loc IN89TK

date 2 : 5.88

band 21

gat 1543

mode J3E

rst 57

QSL via Bureau
or direct to G5LP

mobile/portable from

Tnx:G0HBA GU0ELF GU2FRQ

Bob G1SMI
Roy G0AGE
Tony G0EKD
Roy G4TTX
Dave G4VID
Martin G4YCD
Lionel G5LP

266—GB0IOS 2/5/88 (M:157)

GREETINGS FROM
NEW ZEALAND
ZL4GB

CONFIRMING
QSO WITH W2OJW

DATE			MODE
Day	Month	Year	
3	12	88	SSB/2
GMT	MHz Band		RST
0857	14		57 +QRM

Rig FT 901 DM
Ant. 18 AVT

PSE QSL TNX

OPERATOR:
DUDLEY CARTER
P.O. BOX 6025
INVERCARGILL
NEW ZEALAND
Q.T.H:
Southland Branch 37

NZ
A R
T

267—ZL4GB 3/12/88 (R:158)

MUKACHEVO UKRAINE USSR OBL63

- UB4DXX — club contest call
- RB5DX — Alex
- ☒ UT5DK — Serge

TO RADIO	DATE	UTC	MHZ	RS	2-WAY	QSL
W2OJW	23.10.86	15.36	21	59 55	SSB	PSE

256—UT5DK 10/23/86 (N:157)

UKRAINE USSR
KAMENETS-PODOLSKY
ZONE 16 OBL O79

UB5TCS

VY73! or ALEXANDR ZALIZNIAK
UB 5-O79-237 ex. RB5TCN

TO RADIO	DATE	GMT	BAND MHZ	2 WAY	RS-T
W2OJW	27 10 86	15 47	1,8,3,5,7,14,21,28	☒ SSB ☐ CW	57

JERRY PSE·QSL·TNX VIA P.O. BOX 88, MOSKOW USSR

257—UB5TCS 10/27/86 (N:157)

4U1ITU

ITU HEADQUARTERS, GENEVA

260—4U1ITU 2/24/87 (M:157)

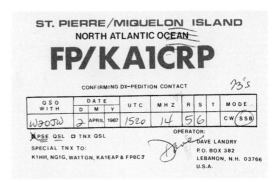

ST. PIERRE/MIQUELON ISLAND
NORTH ATLANTIC OCEAN

FP/KA1CRP

CONFIRMING DX-PEDITION CONTACT 73's

QSO WITH	DATE D	M	Y	UTC	MHZ	R	S	T	MODE
W2OJW	2	APRIL	1987	1520	14	5	6		CW (SSB)

☒ PSE QSL ☐ TNX QSL

OPERATOR:
DAVE LANDRY
SPECIAL TNX TO: P.O. BOX 382
K1HH, NG1G, WA1TGN, KA1EAP & FP8CJ LEBANON, N.H. 03766
U.S.A.

261—FP/KA1CRP 4/2/87 (E:156)

ZONE 28   BULGARIA   QTH BURGAS

LZ1-M-334

WKD DIPOLE RX 15-830s ANT Dipole

TO RADIO	DATE	GMT	MHZ	RS/T	2 WAY
W2OJW	30.10.87	14.20	21.222	55	SSB

PSE/TNX QSL via p.o.box 830 SOFIA
OR DIRECT via p.o.box 394 BURGAS   73'OP

264—LZ1M334 10/30/87 (N:157)

Grand Cayman Island

Arja Nyman   Jan Hubach

ZF2KY   ZF2KZ

OH8BJW   OH1ZAA/FO5ZA/IIII07/PA5CF.N

Grand Cayman

West Bay   North Side   East End

50MHz
ZF2KZ
beacon
EK99HG
locator   George Town   Bodden Town

Special thanks to Rosaleen and Roger Corbin, ZF1RC

265—ZF2KZ 2/24/83 (G:156)

WAZ 15   LATVIJA   OBL 037

UQ2GJN

TO RADIO W2OJW
CFM 2 WAY SSB QSO
DATE 21.03.88 UT 16-35
BAND 21 MC RST 59
LOC : KO26AW
PSE TNX QSL
VIA P.O. BOX 88
MOSCOW USSR

RIGA

OP OSKARS 73! Oreg

268—UQ2GJN 3/21/88 (N:157)

ESTONIA

RR2RN

ZONE 15   REIN KOLK
U-REG 083   ex ur2rkb

269—RR2RN 3/24/88 (N:157)

270—YC0UNJ 4/15/88 (Q:158)

271—JA9AA 4/20/88 (Q:158)

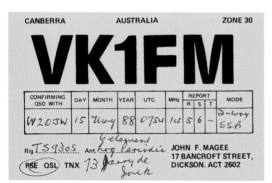

274—VK1FM 5/15/88 (R:158)

275—YC9VGJ 6/3/88 (R:158)

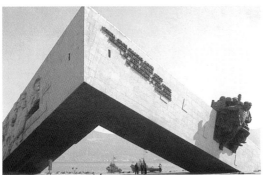

272—UAO112 4/20/88 (P:157)

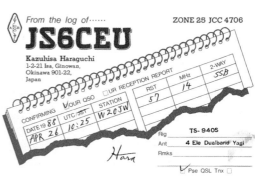

273—JS6CEU 4/26/88 (Q:158)

276—JA8IXM 8/8/88 (Q:158)

277—LX1CC 9/23/88 (M:157)

Father Kevin Burke is a British missionary who has lived on several islands in Western Polynesia.

Vava'u is one of the three island groups that make up the Tongan. It is an archipelago of some 70 coral islands, far taller than Tongatapu, the bigger and more inhabited island to the south.

Legend has it that a mythical hero named Maui pulled both islands out of the sea but put more effort into Vava'u so it rises 200 yards out of the sea and towers over its neighbor. The spirit of one-upsmanship endures on the island. Vava'uns are known as larger-than-life characters, boastful, colorful, with a Texan sense of superiority. They are also overwhelmingly Christian, an apparent testament to Father Burke's skill.

Incidentally, this is the humblest of QSL cards, simply a picture postcard with the call number written in ballpoint pen.

ETHNIC UNREST IN THE BALTIC
REPUBLICS

278—A35KB 10/2/88 (N:155)

Catholic Church - Fungamisi
Vava'u Tonga Islands.

A 35 KB

Confirming our QSO

DATE   2 OCT '88

TIME   0755 - 0816

FREQ   14155

MODE   USB

Sorry, Jerry, didn't note your RST
but good copy. Photo obsolete, new
QTH above tin roof foreground

382 73's Kevin.

278—A35KB (BACK)

Imprimerie M. LESCUYER et Fils
139, cours Albert Thomas — Lyon

MR F.G. POWELL W2OJW

297 COUNTY CLUB DR.

ORADELL   NJ 07649

U.S.A.

Tonga   Acanthurus leucosternon   32s

ARMENIAN EARTHQUAKE, OVER
150,000 KILLED

TERRORISTS EXPLODE PAN AM
FLIGHT 103 OVER LOCKERBIE,
SCOTLAND

10/88   12/88   **192**

AMATEUR RADIO STATION

LZ1KBR

QTH BREZNIK

BULGARIA-ZONE 20

279—LZ1KBR 10/18/88 (N:157)

3W8DX
3W8CW

VIETNAM OPERATION
October 23-November 28, 1988

280—3W8DX 11/22/88 (Q:158)

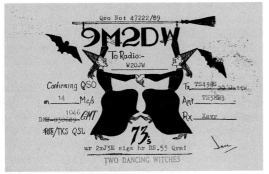

281—9M2DW 3/6/89 (Q:158)

VU7JX : THE LACCADIVES

282—VU7JX 3/22/89 (P:157)

280—3W8DX

The only reference to Vietnam in the collection. Three Hungarians, led by Zoltan Szoke of Budapest, spent a month on this DXpedition, transmitting from various spots in the former war zone.

281—9M2DW

Two dancing witches appear on Tan Bin Hussain's QSL card from Johore, Malaysia.

282—VU7JX

Four Indian hams were on this DXpedition to the Bangaram Island Resort in the Laccadives. The men were from Bangalore, the Silicon Valley of India, home to the world's largest collection of engineers, many of whom are radio amateurs.

AYATOLLAH KHOMEINI
SENTENCES SALMAN RUSHDIE TO
DEATH FOR OFFENSIVE BOOK

EXXON VALDEZ POURS
11 MILLION GALLONS OF CRUDE
OIL INTO ALASKA'S PRINCE
WILLIAM SOUND

Revillagigedo Islands are located 450 miles off the coast of Mexico in the Pacific Ocean. The archipelago consists of three small islands and two adjacent rocks. The island of Socorro is 24 miles long and 9 miles wide and manned by a small military garrison. Europeans had always considered XF4 a mysterious place and only a handful had made contact with the island before. This DXpedition was set up to permanently change the situation. The Beechcraft plane touched down on Socorro's short runway and disgorged eight hams and 6,600 pounds of gear and supplies. The team, from Mexico, Finland, Japan, and the US, set up camp on top of a volcano and fired up the Honda generator. By the time the trip was over, they had logged 47,943 contacts and trained the island's commander to operate the gear they left behind for him. A new link in the chain was forged and Revillagigedo was permanently on the air.

For centuries, the Banaban people lived in peace on their little Pacific island. The location was too remote to be of much interest to anyone, until 1900, when the Pacific Islands Phosphate Company discovered lime phosphate. The Banabans, ignorant of the true value of the deposits, signed away the rights to their island for 50 pounds sterling for the next 999 years. After this deception, the Banabans were shunted to a corner of their little island. They were dealt another blow when the Japanese exiled them all to work camps in Fiji during World War II.

In 1980, mining came to an end, and the island was returned to its original inhabitants, but hardly in its original condition. Most of what was once 1,500 acres of lush tropical land had been mined and devastated, a junk heap of 80-foot limestone pinnacles and massive piles of rusting mining machinery. A couple of hundred Banabans try to eke out a traditional lifestyle amongst the ruins of old company buildings.

When the mines were active, the island was known as "Ocean Island" and was a regular source of ham radio transmissions. Australian hams set up a DXpedition to reconnect the island with the rest of the world and begin to alert people to the calamity its natives had endured. Bob and Jim enlisted many contributors for clearance, gear, transportation, and support, then managed to log 27,200 contacts.

SOVIETS FINISH PULLING OUT OF AFGHANISTAN

XF4L-AIRSTRIP

OPERATING SITES

ICOM
First in Communications

EUDXF

NORTHERN CALIFORNIA
DX FOUNDATION, INC.

REVILLAGIGEDO 1989

XF4L

283—XF4L 4/16/89 (I:156)

T33JS

ZONE 31
0.52S/169.35E

BANABA ISLAND

284—T33JS 5/19/89 (R:158)

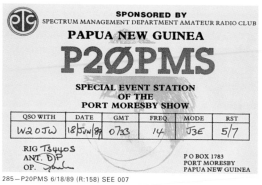

285—P20PMS 6/18/89 (R:158) SEE 007

287—HS1BV 6/28/89 (Q:158)

THOUSANDS OF STUDENTS
KILLED IN CHINA'S TIANANMEN
SQUARE

285—P20PMS

This was Jerry's second contact with Port Moresby. Jerry had made his first DX contact 60 years before.

286—VK8RG

This was the final card Jerry needed to complete his collection of VK contacts. He had now worked all the Australian States plus New Guinea and Antarctica.

VK8RG

RICK K. GALE
21 FORREST CRESCENT
ALICE SPRINGS, NT
AUSTRALIA 0870

286—VK8RG 6/21/89 (R:158)

ZS8MI
MARION ISLAND 1989/90

NORTHERN CALIFORNIA · DX FOUNDATION, INC.

OPERATOR: PETER SYKORA

288—ZS8MI 6/28/89 (P:157)

289—ZS1IS 9/29/89 (N:157)

CIVIL WAR IN ARMENIA AND
AZERBAIJAN

Marion Island is a volcanic island in the southern Indian Ocean, 1,000 miles southeast of South Africa. A cold and unpleasant place, it was rarely visited by anyone but elephant seals and king penguins. In the nineteenth century, sealers began to use the island as a base for hunting operations, stalking animals with clubs and guns. They would boil seal blubber in large try-pots on the beach and harvest seal fur and penguin skins for gloves.

After a century, the seal population had been so depleted that the hunters abandoned the island. In 1947, the South African government took possession of Marion and built a meteorological station. Ever since, scientists have been the island's only human inhabitants, studying the weather and the animal population.

At the time of Jerry's contact with Petr, the base was undergoing one of the few notable events in its history: the Great Cat War. When the station was set up in the late 1940s, the scientists were plagued by the mice that had first immigrated aboard the nineteenth-century sealing ships. To counter the infestation, five cats were released on the island. Soon their descendants became feral and their numbers exploded.

By the 1980s, there were 4,000 cats, which were decimating the local bird population. The scientists released a specific feline disease called panleucopenia, then followed up with nocturnal hunting expeditions. Armed with spotlights and 12-bore shotguns, teams of scientists spent their summer nights culling almost 1,000 cats. Petr and his colleagues then set traps to clean up the stragglers and, after 20 years, bagged the last feral cat in 1991.

PAKISTAN
ZONE 21

AP2-JZB

Confirming QSO with			W2-OJW			
DAY	MONTH	YEAR	UTC	MZH	RST	2-WAY
30 TH	OCTOBER	1989	2054	21.334	43	SSB

C/o P. O. BOX 8507

Tnx for QSL & $ enclosed. Nice meeting you. 73 BoB

PSE QSL TNX
73 : BOB
QTH : Karachi

290—AP2-JZB 10/30/89 (P:157)

CENTRAL AFRICAN REPUBLIC
KEMBE

TL8HW

CQ ZONE 36   **ITU ZONE 47**

QSO WITH	CONFIRMING QSO						
	DAY	MONTH	YEAR	UTC	MHz	RST	2 WAY
W2OJW	15	Nov.	'89	1645	21.33		SSB

WB4LFM-QSL Manager

73. Paul TNX QSL

BAPTIST MISSIONARY
TRACY HULL

292—TL8HW 11/15/89 (M:157)

THE YASME ROUND THE WORLD DX-PEDITION

As of Oct 1989 Lloyd and Iris Colvin have worked half of the active amateurs of the world, traveled in 181 countries, made over 1,040,000 QSOs, worked amateurs in 356 countries, received and filed alphabetically 570,000 QSLs (the largest such collection of QSL's in the world), worked DXCC under 100 different calls, and hold 400 awards working from W6KG, W6DOD, W6QL, FA8JD, W6ANS, W6TG, DL4ZB, W6IPF, K7KG, JA2KG, W6KFD, K2CG, J2AHI, W2USA, K4WAB, W7YA, DL4ZBD, J2USA, W6AHI, W7KG, JA2US, W4KE, DL4ZC, KL7KG, WA6DFR, KL7USA, K6WAP, W6BWS/KG6, W4ZEW, KL7DTB, KG6SZ, W6KG/KG6, KC6SZ, KG6SZ/KC6, VR1Z, GD5ACH/W6KG, GD5ACI/WB6QEP, ZB2AX, GC5ACI/WB6QEP, GC5ACH/W6KG, CT3AU, CT2YA, 6W8CD, 5T5KG, ZD3I, 9L1KG, 5L2KG, 9G1KG, TU2CA, 5V1KG, TY2KG, special event station WW6ITU, VR8B, 3D2KG, C21NI, FK0KG, YJ8KG, W6KG/AJ3, VP2VDJ, VP2EEQ, PJ8KG, W6QL/VP2A, VP2MAQ, KG4KG, W6QL/6Y5, ZF2CI, W6KG/TI5, HR0QL, VP1KG, J3ABV, VP2SAX, J6LOO, J7DBB, VP2KAH, HI6XQL, W6KG/SV9, W6QL/SV5, W6KG/4X, FG0FOL/FS, FG0FOK, FM0FOL, FY0FOL, 8P6QL, 9Y4KG, W6QL/8R1, W6KG/PZ1, W6QL/PJ2, J20DU, G5ACI/AA, W6KG/A4, W6KG/A7, HZ1AB, 9K2QL, JY8KG, W6QL/HK3, W6KG/HK0, W6QL/HC1, W6KG/HC8, 4T4WCY, W6KG/CP6, W6QL/ZP5, W6KG/CE0, W6QL/CE0, KL7DTB/6, KX6SZ, KX6SZ/E, W6KG/ZS, ZS3/W6QL, 7P8KG, 3D6QL, W6QL/Z2, A25/W6KG, 9J2LC, G0/W6KG, F/W6QL, FR/W6QL, FH/W6KG, D68QL, S79KG, 8Q7QL, and 524KG, XE2GKG, 9N5QL, W6KG/4S7, YB0AQL, W6KG/5B4, U3WRW/W6KG, U3WRW/W6QL, UZ3AWA/W6KG, UZ3AWA/W6QL, UZ1AWA/W6KG, UZ1AWA/W6QL, UR1RWW/W6KG, UR1RWW/W6QL, UR1RWX/W6KG, UR1RWX/W6QL, UQ1GXX/W6KG, UQ1GXX/W6QL, UP1BWR/W6KG, UP1BWR/W6QL, UP1BWW/W6KG, UP1BYL/W6QL, UC1AWB/W6KG, UC1AWB/W6QL, UT4UXX/W6KG, UT4UXX/W6QL, RT0U/W6KG, RT0U/W6QL, UO4OWA/W6KG, UO4OWA/W6QL, UF7FWO/W6KG, UF7FWO/W6QL, UD7DWB/W6KG, UD7DWB/W6QL, UH9AWE/W6KG, UH9AWE/W6QL, UJ9JWA/W6KG, UJ9JWA/W6QL, UI9AWD/W6KG, UI9AWD/W6QL, UL8NWC/W6KG, UL8NWC/W6QL, UM9MWA/W6KG, UM9MWA/W6QL, ZC4ZR, 9H3JM, W6QL/5N0, 5U7QL, XT2KG.

YASME FOUNDATION

A non-profit organization. All donations are tax-deductible. Officers and Directors are: President - W6KG, Vice President - N7NG, Vice President Emeritus - Danny Weil - W6RGG, Treasurer - W6BSY. Directors: W0MLY, W6QAT, JA8RUZ, OH2BH, VK2HD, K3ZO, K5RC and W6QL. Past Directors: W8EWS, W5NC, W9AC, JA1KSO. Silent Keys: W6AM, KV4AA, G2DC, W4QDZ, W6GN, K4KCV, W4TO, W5IJG. Special DXpeditions: FO0XX, VK2EO, XF4L. YASME OFFICIALS: QSL PRINTING - WA6AHF, PHOTOGRAPHY - W6RVS, QSL MGR. - WA6AKK, RESIDENT AGENT(FLORIDA) - WA4DRU (PREVIOUS W4QM). The YASME FOUNDATION has sponsored more DXpeditions than any other DX organization in the world.

YASME AWARD

A beautiful certificate awarded free on submitting to W0MLY QSLs for QSOs with any 30 calls on this side of QSL, or QSLs from any other calls held by operators listed including all Yasme officials past or present. The Yasme Award Supreme, a beautiful Yasme boat trophy, is awarded free for submitting QSLs from 60 different Yasme calls. Many Yasme officials have participated in other Dx-Peditions and operated under other calls. They all count for the Yasme Awards. List of such additional calls is available from W0MLY.   WA6AHF

291-5U7QL 11/15/89 (L:157)

N3CRH/TJ

YAOUNDE - CAMEROON

Patti Kellogg
Yaounde DOS
Washington, DC 20521-2520

Confirming QSO with: *Gerald*   ☐ Pse QSL Tnx ☐

STATION	MO	DAY	YR	UTC	FREQ	REPORT	MODE
W2OJW	02	08	90	2100	21—	44	TWO WAY SSB

K2QFL Print

293-N3CRH/TJ 2/8/90 (N:157)

On March 21, 1990, Jerry's wife, Mabel died of a heart attack. She had been head dietician at Presbyterian Medical Center in New York City and in her spare time enjoyed painting. Mabel died a month shy of her 80th birthday and had been married to Jerry for 60 years.

At 81, and for the first time in his life, Jerry was alone. But for his ham radio.

Jerry's son Donald said, "Due to ham radio, I was never really overly concerned about my Dad living alone. He was constantly active with his radio. There were "happy hours" in which he would have regularly scheduled sessions. If he wasn't on the air for any reason, his ham radio buddies would call me and have me check him out. This happened only a few times, and when I went to his house to check on him, he was fine, temporarily engaged in some other activity."

Three weeks after the funeral, Jerry made the next QSO in his collection.

294—VK9TR

Willis Island is in the Coral Sea, a couple of hundred miles off the coast of Queensland. The only activity on the 15-acre atoll is an Australian weather station that was set up in 1921 and is used today to release and track weather balloons. The four full-time weather observers who staff the facility are completely isolated except for their HF radio and the occasional emergency airdrop. The other inhabitants are a huge flock of booby birds whose eggs litter the beaches and paths.

295—AH3C/KH5J

This month-long DXpedition began in Hawaii as the team set sail for Jarvis Island, 2,400 miles away. Jarvis is a small flat coral atoll with a desert climate, no trees, and brutal sunshine. The only inhabitants of this National Wildlife Refuge are close to a million seabirds of a dozen species.

In the late 1850s Hawaiian laborers were brought in to toil for over 30 years, digging away at one of America's richest guano mines (thanks, birds!). Quarries, rock piles, and tramways still remain from the period. After Jarvis's resources were depleted, the island was abandoned for 50 years.

In 1938, the US colonized Jarvis, along with Baker and Howland Islands (see also 359—AH1A), with Hawaiian young men. Each spent six months on Jarvis, taking weather observations, fishing, building a small community of shacks, planning an airplane runway, and operating their ham radios. At the start of World War II, a Japanese submarine shelled the island, killing three men. The survivors were evacuated and Jarvis was again abandoned to the birds until eight DXers showed up on their 71-foot boat. These visitors were from Japan, the Pacific, the US, and Finland, and made 55,000 contacts from their camp.

294—VK9TR 4/6/90 (R:158)

295—AH3C/KH5J 4/22/90 (M:155) SEE 359

7 0 1 A A

296—701AA 5/6/90 (O:157)

KA2IJ

**USCG LORAN STATION
IWO JIMA, JAPAN**

298—KA2IJ 6/19/90 (Q:158) SEE 144

CONWAY REEF
1990

3D2AM

297—3D2AM 5/25/90 (N:155) SEE 295

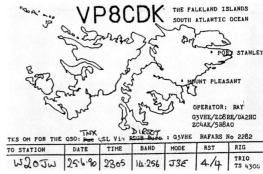

VP8CDK

THE FALKLAND ISLANDS
SOUTH ATLANTIC OCEAN

PORT STANLEY

MOUNT PLEASANT

OPERATOR: RAY
G3VHE/ZD8RE/DA2HC
ZC4AK/5R8AO

TKS OM FOR THE QSO: ~~Pse~~ QSL Via ~~RSGB Buro~~. : G3VHE RAFARS No 2282

TO STATION	DATE	TIME	BAND	MODE	RST	RIG
W2OJW	25.6.90	2305	14.256	J3E	4/4	TRIO TS 430S

299—VP8CDK 6/25/90 (N:156) SEE 361

296—701AA

701AA is a group card from several royal Kuwait hams including Prince Yousuf Al-Sabah (9K2CS) and the head of the Kuwait Amateur Radio Society, Mohamed A. Al-Holi, 9K2DR.

297—3D2AM

Conway Reef is located some 300 miles southeast of Fiji. A lonely place, the reef is made up of a small sandbar with an overall length of less than 400 feet and a surrounding reef a mile in diameter. En route, this DXpedition encountered disaster when their 66-foot schooner lost its engine, generator, and toilet facilities and the group had to reach their destination by sail. (Much of this group had spoken to Jerry earlier from a DXpedition from Jarvis Island, see also 259—AH3C/KH5J.)

Mother Nature continued to conspire against them. Conway is unfortunately infested with tiny ticks that decided to nest in the most sensitive areas of the team's bodies.

They reported: "Life on a DXpedition can be rugged and austere—maybe more so if you have lost your cooking utensils somewhere along the line. Two major rainstorms washed our tents down, leaving all the gear soaking wet and off the air but 3D2AM recovered for 45,000 QSOs with the help of Mother Nature."

INVENTION OF THE WORLD WIDE WEB

GORBACHEV WINS NOBEL PEACE PRIZE

300 — TN1AT

REPUBLIQUE POPULAIRE DU CONGO

WAZ ZONE : 36   ITU ZONE : 52

TN1AT

☒

□ TN0A   □ TN8NU

André TSOUELE   BRAZZAVILLE

QSL VIA F6FNU, P. O. BOX 14, F-91291 ARPAJON Cédex (FRANCE)

CORDIALES 73'
DE BRAZZAVILLE ANDRE

RADIO	DATE	UTC	MHZ	RST	2 WAY
W2OJW	29690	23½	14	59 ~~599~~	SSB CW 3

300 — TN1AT 6/29/90 (N:157)

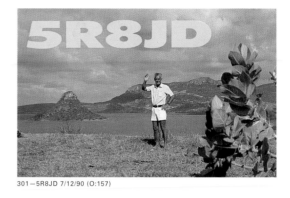

301 — 5R8JD 7/12/90 (O:157)

302 — AH9AC

WAKE ISLAND

"Paradise of the Pacific"

AH9AC

CALL	DATE	UTC	MHZ	MODE	RST
W2OJW	31-7-90	1115	14	2xSSB	33

73

LAT 19° 17'N
LONG 166° 36'E

TOM RUSSELL
301 W. MAIN STREET #10
HYANNIS, MA 02601

QSL MANAGER i8 YCP

ZONEZ 31

302 — AH9AC 7/31/90 (R:158)

ITU 56   WALLIS and FUTUNA.   WAZ 32

A.R.A.N.C Clubmembers DXpedition : 13th to 20th september 1990.
Box 3956 Noumea, NEW CALEDONIA

303 — ITU56 9/14/90 (R:158)

304 — VP8CDJ

50°.00 STH.   **SOUTH GEORGIA**   38°.02 W.

BRITISH ANT. SURVEY. BIRD ISL. STH. ATLANTIC.

VP8CDJ

CONFIRMING QSO WITH

STATION	D	M	YR	GMT	MHZ	2xSSB
W2OJW	24	9	90	2312	14	52

QSL MANAGER:
GM4KLO, MIKE
TNX ☑ PSE □ QSL   73 Mike

OPERATOR:
GORDON

304 — VP8CDJ 9/24/90 (P:157)

305 — VP8BXK 9/27/90 (P:157)

306 — V85RM

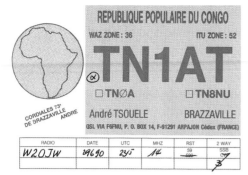

BRUNEI

9M6

DARUSSALAM

OP. RUSLI MAH MOOD

9M8

9V1

EAST MALAYSIA
WAZ ZONE 28 - ITU ZONE 54

o V85RM

o 9M8MR

o V85ZM

ZULKAIDAH MANAP

YB

INDIAN OCEAN

SEA OF CHINA

CQ ZONE : 28
ITU ZONE : 54

YB

RADIO	DATE				RST	2 WAY
*W2OJW	101290	2215				
	14	SSB/59				

QSL VIA F6FNU, BP 14, F-91291 ARPAJON CEDEX (FRANCE)

306 — V85RM 10/12/90 (Q:158)

Greetings from Sudan
ST2YD

307 — ST2YD 10/18/90 (N:157)

301—5R8JD

This cheery fellow on a cliff overlooking Madagascar in the Malagasy Republic, is Jean-Paul Delpierre, a Frenchman and member of the Lions Club.

308—ZK3KY 10/18/90 (M:155)

311—CY9CF

This was a French Canadian DXpedition to Saint Paul Island off Canada's east coast, also known as the "Graveyard of the Gulf" for its high seas and terrible weather. Worsening conditions cut short the plans of the three hams to four and half days. Nonetheless they managed to make 17,139 QSOs to 145 countries.

314—HK0TU

Two previous DXpeditions to Malpelo had resulted in severe injuries. The coast is entirely ringed with treacherous cliffs swept by large waves in a sea full of sharks. The Colombian League of Radio Amateurs carefully planned and organized the trip well in advance, then 15 hams climbed the rock face and installed their gear. Over five days, they contacted tens of thousands of hams in over 150 countries.

JAN MAYEN

JX7DFA

CQ Zone 40   ITU Zone 18

Operator : LA7DFA, Per Einar Dahlen

CONFIRMING QSO:	DAY-MONTH-YEAR			UTC	MHz	RS(T)	2 WAY
W2OJW	23	10	90	2115	14	59	CW/SSB

Jan Mayen is a Norwegian arctic island situated 71°N, 8°W between Norway and Greenland. The island is volcanic, with the active volcano Beerenberg (2277 m.a.s.l.) last erupting in 1970.

QSL SPONSORED BY LA-DX-GROUP

QSL Mngr. LA2KD, Annar Kjernsvik. Verified by: Per

309—JX7DFA 10/23/90 (M:157)

KC6JC
POHNPEI, E. CAROLINE IS.

VL3JC

FR. JOSEPH A. CAVANAGH, SJ

PATS, P. O. Box 39
Pohnpei, FM, Caroline Is. 96941

TO RADIO	DATE	UTC	RST	MHz	2x	QSL
W2OJW	10-24-90	1148	54	14	SSB	PSE TNX

310—KC6JC 10/24/90 (R:158)

TY1DX
BENIN

313—TY1DX 10/26 (M:157)

HK0TU

MALPELO I., Colombia

314—HK0TU 11/5/90 (I:156)

Father Marshall Moran was a Jesuit priest. He arrived in India in 1929 and became one of the first foreigners allowed into Nepal, which had been completely shut off for a century. He helped set up and run three schools for thousands of Nepali students, many of whom went on to play major roles in Nepal's government and industry.

For 40 years, Moran was an ardent ham radio operator, and he had many friends worldwide. He assisted in medical emergencies in Nepal, ship evacuations at sea, a storm-stricken expedition in Antarctica, and even delivered an Easter Sunday sermon by ham radio to a group in Antarctica. His key went silent on April 13, 1992.

311—CY9CF 10/25/90 (E:156)

312—TQ2X 10/26/90 (M:157)

315—9N1MM 11/6/90 (P:157)

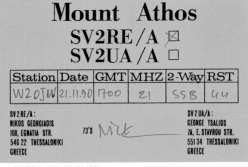

316—SV2RE/A 11/21/90 (N:157)

On August 2, 1990 Iraq invaded Kuwait, leading to Operation Desert Storm. During the next six months, Jerry spoke to people across the region. He contacted hams in Dubai, Sudan, Bahrain, Israel, Saudi Arabia, even Tehran. More than any other conflict of the twentieth century, Jerry's radio gave him personal access to the Gulf War.

A contact made during the increasing tension in the Middle East following the Iraqi invasion of Kuwait, the day after the UN Security Council passed a resolution authorizing force if Iraq didn't withdraw.

As Jerry was speaking to his new friend, Irma Meshellany in Beirut, President Bush invited Iraqi foreign minister Tariq Aziz to Washington and offered to send Secretary of State James Baker to Baghdad. Jerry's call met with far more success.

OD5MM

WAZ 20
ITU 39

BEIRUT

LEBANON

IRMA MISHELLANY
P.O. Box 184
JOUNIEH / LEBANON

317—OD5MM 11/30/90 (N:157)

A61AC

ZONE 21   Dubai   U.A.E.

318 — A61AC 12/17/90 (O:157)

S T Ø D X

Southern Sudan
Dennis Goedraad

320 — ST0DX 1/15/91 (N:157)

7Z1AB

DESERT STORM   **SAUDI ARABIA**

319—7Z1AB 1/2/91 (O:157)

VE4ANM/4U

CANADIAN CONTINGENT
UNITED NATIONS DISENGAGEMENT
OBSERVER FORCE
GOLAN HEIGHTS

Op. *Tom*

P.O.BOX 386
TIBERIAS 14103 ISRAEL

THIS STATION LOCATED IN
SYRIA, BUT AT PRESENT IS
ISRAELI OCCUPIED
THIS CARD COUNTS
AS SYRIA (Y.K.)

CALL	DATE	GMT	FREQ	MODE	RST
W2OJW	Jan 29/91	21:55	14 MHz.	2×SSB	5/4

321—VE4ANM/4U 1/29/91 (N:157)

318—A61AC

This was another contact on the front lines of the Gulf War, this one with Dr. M. Hamdan in Dubai, United Arab Republic.

319—7Z1AB

The club station of the US Embassy Amateur Radio Society in Riyadh had three HF positions and an array of antennas on the roof; many expats gathered there to operate every Wednesday evening. They had little choice. A Saudi ham license is a privilege reserved for members of the Al-Saud royal family.

No doubt Jerry's conversation with 7Z1AB touched on the increasing tension in the region. There were only a couple of weeks left until the deadline set by the UN Security Council. Despite discussions between Baghdad and Washington, the threat of war was mounting each day.

320—ST0DX

Like ET2A, this DXpedition was run by a member of the 256 DX Group. The hams found themselves in the middle of civil war–torn Africa; adding to the tension, an all-out war in the Middle East was just days away. Sudan faced famine after two consecutive years of drought while the Gulf War sent home thousands of workers from Kuwait. A new code of Islamic law instituted amputation, stoning, and other harsh measures. Due to Sudan's human rights record and support of Iraq, international food relief was slow to come. The civil war and ensuing famines produced over a million casualties.

Despite the threat to his personal safety, Dennis Goedraad remained in southern Sudan, carrying on the ham tradition of providing a connection to the outside world in a time of emergency.

321—VE4ANM/4U

This contact came less than two weeks after US warplanes first attacked Baghdad, Kuwait and other military targets in Iraq. While Scud missiles were being aimed at Israel, Jerry was speaking to someone in the thick of the conflict.

Israel has occupied this region of southwest Syria since the Six Day War in 1967. However, after Syria's surprise attack during the Yom Kipur War in 1973, Mount Hermon was divided among Lebanon, Israel, Syria, and several UN demilitarized zones. UN peacekeeping forces have been on the Golan Heights ever since.

After the Gulf War, Syrian-Israeli peace talks finally began but in the decade or more since have yet to reach any meaningful resolution.

323—EP2HZ

Jerry had the chance to speak to another ham on the front lines of the Gulf War, this time in the capital of Iran, Iraq's longtime enemy.

324—ZL0AAD/ZL7

Hungarian Eli Bielek is a freelance documentary filmmaker who also exports black pearls while traveling the South Pacific on various DXpeditions. Besides this trip to Chatham, he visited Niue, South Cook, Banaba, and East and West Kiribati, making thousands of contacts and videotaping his adventures.

325—A92FL

This card commemorates Operation Desert Shield, the opening salvo of the Gulf War. It comes from Sheik Isa Air Base in Bahrain where many of the 500,000 US troops gathered in the gulf. The next day, longtime ham King Hussein of Jordan, would lash out against the US bombardments and turn his support to Iraq.

327—VE7GCK/A7

Though not yet directly involved in the Gulf War at this point, Darcy Bens was a communicator in the Royal Canadian Navy stationed in Doha, Qatar.

NEW "NO CODE" TECHNICIAN CATEGORY LICENSE MEANS HAMS CAN GET ON THE AIR WITHOUT MORSE CODE PROFICIENCY

322—XQ0X 1/30/91 (M:156)

323—EP2HZ 1/31/91 (O:157)

324—ZL0AAD/ZL7 2/1/91 (R:158)

STATE OF BAHRAIN

A92FL

OPERATION DESERT SHIELD

SHEIK ISA AIR BASE

Rig - Harris GRC 193, 400 watts   MARK BITTERLICH

☐ Pse QSL   ☑ Tnx   73

QSO WITH	DATE	GMT	MHz	RST	2 WAY
W2OJW	5 Feb 91	1720	28	3/3	SSB

325—A92FL 2/5/91 (O:157)

326—ZK2XB 2/6/91 (N:155)

DARCY BENS
DOHA, QATAR

"CANADA DRY ONE"

VE7GCK/A7

TO RADIO: W2OJW

This confirms our 2xSSB QSO
91/02/12 at 2108Z on 14,160 Mhz.
Your signals RS 58

QSL Received TNX. 73 - Darcy.

327—VE7GCK/A7 2/12/91 (O:157)

328—9U5QL 2/15/91 (N:157) SEE 369

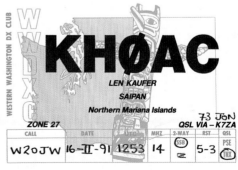

329—KH0AC 2/16/91 (R:158)

To Radio W2OJW

DATE D M Y	TIME UTC	FREQ MHz	SIGS R S T	MODE
16-2-91	1147	14.226	5 X 7 5 X 9	SSB

RIG TS 930 S ANT ☑ VERT ☐ BEAM ☐ INVT VEE
TS 130 S

Confirming
QSO with

Y J 8 R N

CQ ZONE 32 — ITU ZONE 56

LOCATOR - RH 42 JQ

IOTA# OC-35

VILA

ROD NEWELL
BOX 905
PORT VILA
VANUATU

330 — YJ8RN 2/16/91 (R:158)

DXING AND DXPEDITIONS

DX means "long distance" and hams who specialize in contacting stations in distant countries are called DXers. Special receivers, powerful antennas, and lots of patience and experience help them pull in hams on the other side of the planet. The more distant and obscure the contact, the greater an accomplishment it represents. DXers "collect" countries and try to accumulate QSL cards from as many as possible. These cards are used as proof to earn special certificates from organizations like the ARRL.

When a country has no amateur radio operators at all, a group of hams will mount a DXpedition and travel to operate their radios there for a few days. Hams around the world get advance word that such a trip is being arranged and will get a chance to make contact with a brand new location.

On May 29, 1992, Jerry sat in his basement in Oradell, waiting to pick up a signal from a one-man DXpedition to a lonely chunk of rock thousands of miles away. Then, in a fleeting contact, Jerry was allowed to vicariously share an adventure that had taken years of preparation and experience.

DXpedition to MARKET REEF

When Leif Lindgren was 16, he took off to sea and saw the world. At 19, he was drafted into the Swedish navy and became a radio operator on an icebreaker, ODEN 60-61. Someone suggested he might be interested in becoming a ham, but after all that time in the radio room, sending and receiving telegrams, Leif wasn't interested. He'd had quite enough of tapping out code with a telegraph key. But at 30, Leif caught the ham bug and took his first licensing exam. By the next year, he was ready for a more advanced license that let him onto other frequencies. Soon, Leif had his A license, joined the S.S.A. and the ARRL and today holds an Honor Roll plaque for his DX accomplishments.

He says, "The ham radio is a wonderful way of making friends all over the globe. The operators can be from a king to a garbage man. We all share the same interest." Indeed, Leif had three conversations with JY1, King Hussein of Jordan, each of which was confirmed by a

FIG. 28
(previous)
Leif's gear included
this vertical anten-
na HS-VK5, 5 band
and some dipoles.
He also had a 1kw
amplifier and an
ICOM radio, while
Peter used a
Kenwood.

QSL card from the king. The king was, by all reports, a very nice man and an avid DXer who also staged his own DXpedition.

Leif has made many friends over his 30 years on the air. One of his friends in the US suggested that he set up a DXpedition to Aaland Island, a Swedish province of Finland that is its own DX country, OH0. With several Swedish friends, he took the trip and made many contacts, one of which was a long conversation on 75 meters with Peter, SM0NZZ. The two hams stayed in touch and became good friends.

Soon after, Peter and Leif started planning a new DXpedition to Market Reef, a tiny dot of rock, two and a half hours west of Aaland, so small it can't be found on most maps. Leif's friends in the US were very excited, as Market Reef is also a separate and very hard-to-get DX country. The trip was a last hurrah for Peter who was soon to be married; the two packed enough food and gear to last for a week.

FIG. 29

The lighthouse with its solar panels and the main generator building

MARKET REEF

SMØFWW/OJØ

OPERATOR: LEIF LINDGREN (LB)

CONFIRMING QSO WITH	DATE			UTC	MHz	RST	MODE 2-WAY
	DAY	MONTH	YEAR				
W2OJW	29	May	92	2246	14	3-3	SSB

Confirmed by
Alan E. Strauss
WA4JTK

☐ PSE QSL ☑ TNX QSL   A W4MPY QSL

FIG. 30

Leif Lindgren's
QSL card from the
DXpedition to
Market Reef

Oradell, Bergen County, New Jersey 07649
297 COUNTRY CLUB DRIVE
SMØFWW/OJ UR 20 SSB SIGS W RK 29 May 92 R 3-3 T
(1045 Z)

W2OJW

500 WATTS   RIG TS 830 ANT MiniQuad
TNX QSO New Country LV.
PSE QSL   GERALD POWELL, Opr.

FIG. 31

Jerry Powell's
QSL card received
by Leif

FIG. 32

Leif's generator
sits next to the
massive concrete
blocks that support
the buildings on
Market Reef.

FIG. 33
(right)
The Market Reef log

Market Reef is only 300 feet long and 200 wide but it has a border running right through it. Half belongs to Finland, the rest to Sweden. As Leif puts it, "The only building in Sweden is the outhouse, hihi." The Finnish half holds a lighthouse built in 1885 by the Russians, who then ruled Finland (FIG. 29). The shipping lanes are full of dangerous rocks, and the Russians took on the fairly Herculean task of building a lighthouse on this remote and barren rock.

The workers built themselves wooden shacks and began to quarry rock to lay the foundation. Before long, a violent storm wiped out the barracks, three men, and all the work that had been done. A revised plan of attack brought rock from Helsinki by ferry, and the new crew bunked aboard ship for a year while completing the work.

Over the years, two more buildings were thrown up on the reef: a shed and a building to house three decrepit and unreliable diesel generators. The buildings are linked to the lighthouse by a rick-

United States of America
Bearing 295 degrees 1p=115
6,398 km to Trenton
DXCC=Cnfm ITU=Cnfm

```
┌────────────────────┐
│ DST  10:37:16      │
│ UTC  09:37:16      │
│ QSOs   21,778      │
│ Order    C1Bk      │
└────────────────────┘
```

              Call: W2OJW
              Date: 05/29/92 May.29, 1992
              Time: 22:46   11:46 pm DST
         Frequency: 14.2265   20 Meters
       Report Sent: 33
   Report Received: 33   CQ Zone: 05
              Name: GERALD   ITU Zone: 08
               QTH: ORADELL, NJ   Cont: North America
          QSL Sent: Yes   US State: New Jersey
      QSL Received: Yes   County: NJ Bergen
          Emission: USB
             Power: 500
              Code: 005 DJ0/SI8, Market Reef
             Flags: /u1748

U
ENTER SELECTION: Add   Comments Edit Find Global Print
   M = Help   Remove Search Main Menu   E D
```

| 22 | GI | Northern Ireland | GI4WVN | 05/29/92 | 16:44 | 14.243 | USB | 56 | 59 |
|----|-----|------------------|---------|----------|-------|--------|-----|----|----|
| 23 | GM | Scotland | GM0EFT | 05/30/92 | 10:56 | 14.242 | USB | 55 | 58 |
| 24 | GU | Guernsey & Dep. | GU0ALD | 05/29/92 | 00:12 | 7.044 | LSB | 58 | 59 |
| 25 | GW | Wales | GW0DST | 05/29/92 | 09:44 | 14.247 | USB | 58 | 59 |
| 26 | HA | Hungary | HA5DG | 05/30/92 | 10:43 | 14.242 | USB | 56 | 59 |
| 27 | HB | Switzerland | HB9BGV | 05/31/92 | 01:36 | 7.056 | USB | 59 | 59 |
| 28 | HB0 | Liechtenstein | DA1WA/HB0 | 05/28/92 | 15:58 | 21.335 | USB | 51 | 55 |
| 29 | HC | Ecuador | HC1JOL | 05/30/92 | 01:53 | 14.236 | USB | 53 | 53 |
| 30 | HI | Dominican Republic | HI3HBD | 05/29/92 | 04:13 | 14.236 | USB | 55 | 33 |
| 31 | HK | Colombia | HK5DER | 05/28/92 | 04:14 | 14.236 | USB | 55 | 55 |
| 32 | HP | Panama | HP6AYV | 05/28/92 | 05:13 | 14.236 | USB | 45 | 55 |
| 33 | HZ | Saudi Arabia | HZ1TA | 05/29/92 | 16:13 | 14.243 | USB | 55 | 55 |
| 34 | I | Italy | IV3JVJ | 05/29/92 | 00:07 | 7.044 | LSB | 59 | 59 |
| 35 | IS | Sardinia | IS0PFD | 05/28/92 | 17:22 | 14.243 | USB | 53 | 54 |
| 36 | J3 | Grenada | J39CO | 05/28/92 | 03:14 | 14.236 | USB | 53 | 53 |
| 37 | JA | Japan | JA7KQC/4 | 05/29/92 | 16:37 | 14.243 | USB | 33 | 54 |
| 38 | JW | Svalbard | JW5E | 05/28/92 | 10:19 | 14.247 | USB | 59 | 59 |
| 39 | JY | Jordan | JY5IN | 05/28/92 | 00:10 | 14.2265 | USB | 58 | 57 |
| 40 | K | United States of America | K7CRM | 05/30/92 | 00:01 | 14.2265 | USB | 44 | 54 |
| 41 | KL7 | Alaska | KL7AMH | 05/28/92 | 05:08 | 14.236 | USB | 33 | 55 |
| 42 | KP2 | Virgin Islands | KP2AD | 05/28/92 | 15:27 | 21.335 | USB | 52 | 55 |
| 43 | KP4 | Puerto Rico | KP4CKY | 05/28/92 | 02:44 | 14.236 | USB | 53 | 53 |
| 44 | LA | Norway | LA8RFA | 05/29/92 | 04:30 | 14.32 | USB | 59 | 59 |
| 45 | LU | Argentina | LU5FCI | 05/28/92 | 23:11 | 14.2265 | USB | 59 | 59 |
| 46 | LX | Luxembourg | LX1SP | 05/28/92 | 10:07 | 14.247 | USB | 59 | 59 |
| 47 | LZ | Bulgaria | LZ1CC . | 05/29/92 | 15:45 | 14.243 | USB | 58 | 59 |
```

ety iron catwalk and perch above the encroaching icepack on a 20-foot slab of concrete.

A patrol boat ferried Leif, Peter, their provisions, antennas, amplifiers, and radios over to the reef. The going was treacherous and, if the wind had exceeded five miles per hour, they would not have been able to land; the rock is only six feet above sea level.

Though the conditions on the barren rock were rough, the DXpedition was a great success, and the team made several hundred contacts, including W2OJW. At 11:46 P.M., DST, Jerry's voice appeared on the 20-meter band at 14.2265 khz. It had traveled 6,398 kilometers to Market Reef. Much of the operation was fast and didn't allow for extended chats, so Jerry and Leif just managed to establish contact, exchange a few words before they had to move on to the next caller.

Leif recorded the contact with W2OJW on his log. When he returned home, he sent out a QSL card and received one from Jerry and most of the other hams he contacted that day.

Scott Maurice began as a ham in high school and worked nearly 130 countries from his home station. After going to work as a communication specialist for the Defense Department, he began to travel to some of those distant spots he'd only ever visited over the air. He went on to see and operate from Monrovia to Mauritania, Kampuchea to Kenya.

His DXpedition to Addis Ababa wasn't much of a picnic. The country was racked by bloody coups, uprisings, wide-scale drought, and massive refugee problems. Scott arrived at the climax of two decades of civil war against the Stalinist military junta that had deposed Emperor Haile Selassie. The government had been responsible for the torture, murder, and disappearance of tens of thousands of the country's citizens. Fortunately, within months of Scott's visit, the Ethiopian People's Revolutionary Democratic Front established a free-market, multiparty democracy.

Despite the dawn of freedom, to this day there is only one phone and one TV for every 500 people in Ethiopia. Scott's ham radio set remains one of the best ways to communicate with the world.

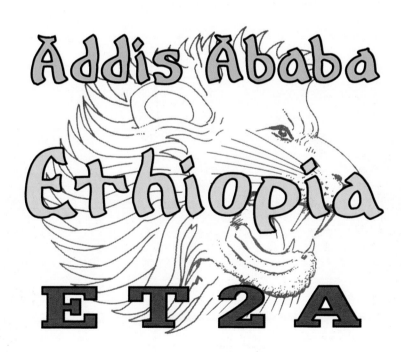

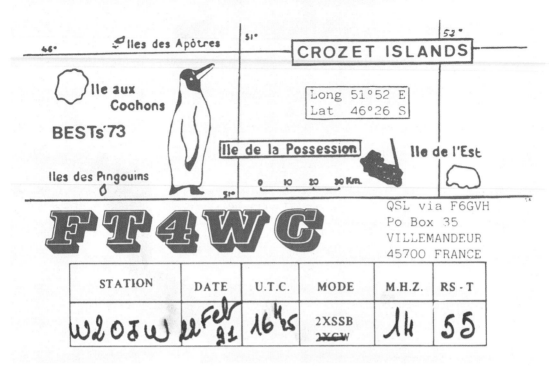

332—FT4WC 2/22/91 (P:157)

334—FT4YD 3/5/91 (P:157)

XFØC

CLARION ISLAND

REVILLAGIGEDO
MEXICO

114.45 N
18.21 W

IOTA: NA-115   GRID SQ.DK 28   CQ 6   ITU 10

333—XF0C 2/23/91 (H:156)

VKØKC ANTARCTICA

DATE	UTC	FREQ.	SIG	MODE	WORKED
3.4.91	1243	20MTR	5+5	2×SSB	W2O5W

335—VK0KC 4/3/91 (P:157)

335—VK0KC

Antarctica doesn't belong to anyone, but about a dozen countries have territorial claims and have established about 40 bases on the continent. There is complete collaboration between the different scientific research stations. The distinguishing factor is that each station adheres to the time zone of its home country, so visitors to other bases can go through abrupt jet lag.

Life in an Antarctica station is tough and lonely. Studies show that after a year staff show similar symptoms to returning POWs. The annals of the frozen continent are replete with stories of people going stircrazy, getting blitzed on home-brew, and attacking each other with various implements. On an Argentine expedition, a doctor, anxious to be shipped home, burnt down his own base. A chess game led one Soviet scientist to axe another. When people freak out, they have to be sequestered in padded cells for months until they can be evacuated after the thaw.

Not all of the nuttiness is pathological. Members of the 300 Club have to jump naked out of a 200-degree (Fahrenheit) sauna and run outside and around the marker for the South Pole where it's generally 100 degrees below. Members of the Vanda Swimming club have broken through the ice of Lake Varda and plunged in, stark naked.

340—ZA1A

Albania was the only Chinese outpost in Europe, sealed off from the rest of the world. After a couple of decades of negotiation with Albanian bureaucrats, an international group managed to get permission for the very first ZA or Albanian ham license. This card commemorates the group effort of Italians, Germans, Americans, Japanese, and Scandinavians who brought in expertise and equipment, and trained a dozen Albanians to plant a new seed for global communications.

AUCKLAND IS, 1991

ZL9DX

336—ZL9DX 5/3/91 (R:158)

SAINT BRANDON ISLAND

3B8CF/3B7

A.R.S. W2OJW DATE 23.9.91
GMT 1915 MHz 21 RST 55 2-WAY SSB Jacky

Op: SEEWOOSANKAR MANDARY VY 73
VQ8CF, VQ8CFB, 3B8CF, 3B7CF, 3B8CF, 3B9CF, VQ9SM, KB1PR
QSL for any of the above to be sent direct to 3B8CF Add: Shastri Road, Candos, Quatre Bornes. MAURITIUS.

339—3B8CF/3B7 9/23/91 (P:157)

Slovenija

YT3CW

WAZ 15
ITU 28
LOC JN76CI

CFM QSO WITH
W2OJW

DATE	GMT	MHz	RST	MODE
26.11.91	16:14	28	57	SSB

RX/TX: FT-767GX
ANT.: 3el.

DR OM Jerry
HPE CUAGN BEST DX PSE QSL TNX

UROŠ HIRCI
GORICA 14
64240 RADOVLJICA

342—YT3CW 11/26/91 (N:157)

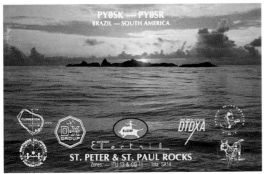

337—PY0SK-PY0SR 5/7/91 (K:156)

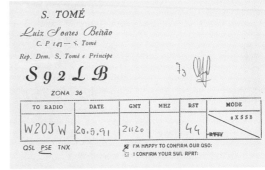

338—S92LB 5/20/91 (M:157)

340—ZA1A 9/23/91 (N:157)

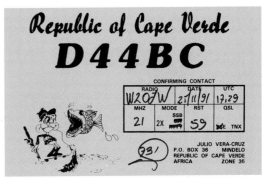

341—D44BC 11/25/91 (L:157)

COMOROS ISLANDS
INDIAN OCEAN

D68JM

343—D68JM 12/6/91 (O:157)

344—9M8FH 1/31/92 (Q:158)

345—YX0AI 2/3/92 (H:156)

LITHUANIA, ESTONIA, AND LATVIA
WIN INDEPENDENCE

FOØ Clipperton Island 1992

346—FO0CI 3/10/92 (I:156)

Clipperton has become legendary among hams as "hard luck island" because so many DXpeditions have had grueling experiences there. It is impossible to land a plane, and access by sea is thwarted by the treacherous reef. Contact is so rare—a couple of days twice every decade or so—that this QSL is much sought after.

The first hams arrived in April 23, 1954 after a terrible journey, fighting against the powerful waves that slam up against the reef. They finally managed to land and establish FO8AJ for just 18 hours and worked 1,100 contacts before they had to evacuate. This DXpedition was a huge event in the amateur radio world, a cover story for ham magazines worldwide. Ever since, Clipperton has been the quintessential place for a DXpedition. After a Franco-Swiss expedition managed to make 29,000 contacts in over a week in 1978, they formed an organization named after the spot, the Clipperton DX Club, whose membership logo can be found on many of the cards in Jerry's collection.

Hams were not the only ones to suffer on Clipperton. It has a rich and tortured history for such a tiny place.

Clipperton Island is two square miles of France 785 miles west of Acapulco, and the only resident mammals are wild pigs. The sole atoll in the Eastern Pacific, it was discovered by Ferdinand Magellan in 1521 but named for John Clipperton, a mutineer and pirate who made it his hideout in 1705. The French first arrived on the island in 1708 and, except for a scientific expedition in the early eighteenth century, did nothing with it until the US scored guano mining rights and began to work the island. The next year, the French annexed Clipperton, which they named Ile de la Possession, claiming it was technically part of French Polynesia. The island was abandoned until 1897 when Mexico took it over, set up a garrison, and sold mining rights to a British company.

Soon 100 men and women lived on the island, supported by supply shipments from the mainland. As the Mexican Revolution between the Zapatistas and the government's troops gained momentum, all provisions for the islanders were cut off, and they were forced to live off coral, sand, crabs, and pigs. By 1917, only three inhabitants were still alive and were rescued by an American ship.

With the intervention of the Pope, the island was returned to France in 1930 but remained unoccupied until the US Navy set up a secret operation there during World War II. Hams, French sailors, Mexican fishermen, and various scientists have been the only visitors since.

347—YA5MM

Igor Petrashko and Nodir Tusoon Zadeh worked out of Soviet-occupied Afghanistan in the early 1990s. They set up in Mazar-e-Sharif, only 50 kilometers from the border of Tajikistan. The area was enormously dangerous; after curfew, any passersby could be shot without warning. The enemy was 30 kilometers away and bombarded continuously. Whoever wished to erect an antenna anywhere was automatically a target of all the warring parties. After paying the "protective duty" to the local rulers, Igor and Nodir put up an antenna and started operating. With remarkable difficulty, they made 32,000 contacts with other hams.

349—3D2AG

On this DXpedition to Fapufa Village on Rotuma Island, Antoine encountered very primitive conditions. With no existing source of electricity, he used a rig that was solar-powered.

350—SM0FWM/050

For the full story on this QSO, see pp. 217–224.

AFGHANISTAN
March 1992

 YA5MM

BY

| UT4UX | UJ8JMM |
| IGOR | NODIR |

347—YA5MM 3/13/92 (O:157)

CQ ZONE 25   IOTA AS-076
ITU ZONE 45   Shikoku Island
JCC-3801   Loc. PM63IT

J R 5 J A Q

OP. **JR5JAQ** MASANOBU YAMAO

QTH. 222-44 Higashihabu Matsuyama-city
     EHIME 791 JAPAN

also JR5JAQ/JD1 1991 APR.
     T32J   1994 DEC.-1995 JAN.

Member of EHIME DX GROUP e-mail NCN98485 @ pcvan.or.jp
         JH5ZCP , JD1YBK   VYA00316 @ niftyserve.or.jp

348—JR5JAQ 3/25/92 (Q:158)

MARKET REEF

SM0FWW/OJ0

OPERATOR: LEIF LINDGREN (LB)

| CONFIRMING QSO WITH | DATE | | | UTC | MHz | RST | MODE 2-WAY |
	DAY	MONTH	YEAR				
W2OJW	29	May	92	2246	14	3-3	SSB

Confirmed by
Alan E. Strauss
WA4JTK

☐ PSE QSL ☑ TNX QSL   A W4MPY QSL

350—SM0FWW/OJ0 5/29/92 (N:157)

351—4J1FS 6/8/92 (N:157)

ROTUMA ISLAND
DXPEDITION

3D2AG/P

IOTA OC-60
CQ 32

TO RADIO: W 2 O J W

DATE	TIME (UTC)	BAND(MHZ)							RST		MODE	
		7	14	18	21	24	28	60	59	599	SSB	CW
22·4. 92	1100		X						X		X	

TNX QSL   73,

ANTOINE D.R.NYEURT
P.O.BOX 14633
SUVA, FIJI
Thanks to Aisake Family and
the kind people of Rotuma

FAPUFA VILLAGE
SOLAR POWERED STN
RIG: FT-757GX/TS600
ANT: CUSHCRAFTA3/4-EL YAGI/DIP

349—3D2AG 4/22/92 (R:158)

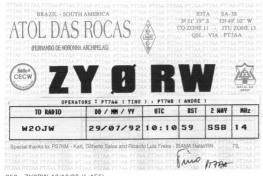

BRAZIL - SOUTH AMERICA   IOTA   SA-38
3° 51' 19" S   33° 49' 10" W

ATOL DAS ROCAS   CQ ZONE 11 · ITU ZONE 13
QSL VIA PT7AA.

(FERNANDO DE NORONHA ARCHIPELAG)

CECW

ZY 0 RW

NATAL D.X GROUP

OPERATORS : PT7AA (TINO) , PT7WB (ANDRE)

TO RADIO	DD / MM / YY	UTC	RST	2 WAY	MHz
W2OJW	29/07/92	10:10	59	SSB	14

Special thanks to: PS7KM - Karl, Gilberto Sales and Ricardo Luis Freire - IBAMA Natal/RN   73,

352—ZY0RW 12/10/92 (L:156)

LA RIOTS AFTER RODNEY KING
VERDICT

REPUBLIC OF CROATIA
9A2PM

| CONFIRMING QSO WITH | DATE | | | UTC | MHz | RST | MODE 2-WAY | QSL |
---	DAY	MONTH	YEAR					
W2OJW	21	9	92	1436	21	56	SSB	TNx

MARKO PAVLIC
S. KRAUTZEKA 91
51000 RIJEKA
CROATIA, EUROPE

QSL MGR.
KA9WON

A WX9X QSL

CQ ZONE 15
ITU ZONE 28
10 X #31737
H.I.DX #744

353—9A2PM 9/21/92 (N:157)

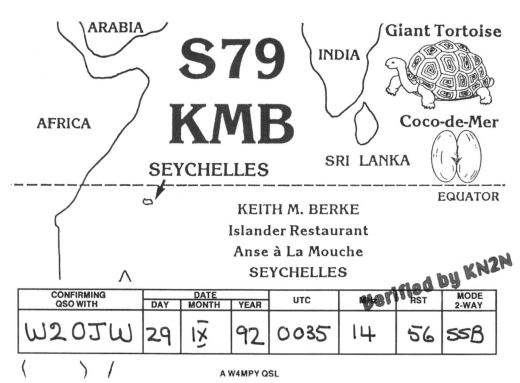

ARABIA

S79
KMB

INDIA

Giant Tortoise

AFRICA

SEYCHELLES

SRI LANKA

Coco-de-Mer

EQUATOR

KEITH M. BERKE
Islander Restaurant
Anse à La Mouche
SEYCHELLES

Verified by KN2N

| CONFIRMING QSO WITH | DATE | | | UTC | MHz | RST | MODE 2-WAY |
---	DAY	MONTH	YEAR				
W2OJW	29	IX	92	0035	14	56	SSB

A W4MPY QSL

354—S79KMB 9/29/92 (O:157)

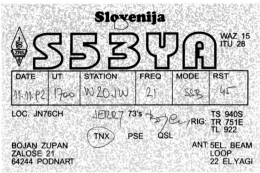

Slovenija

S53YA

WAZ 15
ITU 28

DATE	UT	STATION	FREQ	MODE	RST
11.11.92	1700	W2OJW	21	SSB	45

LOC. JN76CH   73's

TNX   PSE   QSL

RIG: TS 940S
TR 751E
TL 922

BOJAN ZUPAN
ZALOSE 21
64244 PODNART

ANT: 5EL. BEAM
LOOP
22 EL.YAGI

355—S53YA 11/11/92 (N:157)

D68GA
Don Jones

Comoro
Islands

356—D68GA 11/25/92 (O:157)

South Shetland Islands

The 16ᵗʰ Polish Antarctic Expedition

HFØPOL

357—HF0POL 11/25/92 (N:156)

INDEXA

BANGLADESH

S21ZG

TO STATION	CONFIRMING QSO						
	DAY	MONTH	YEAR	UTC	MHz	2-WAY	RST
W2OJW	30	I	93	12/4	14	SSB	33

ERIK BIORCK

358—S21ZG 1/30/93 (P:157)

356—D68GA

This picture is of Don Jones and his Kenwood TS-390 with children from the village of Mitsamouli on the island of Grand Comodore. The Republique Federale Islamique des Comodres is a group of three islands in the Indian Ocean between Mozambique and Madagascar.

Don was on a one-man DXpedition, hosted by a local ham, Dr. John Mustol (D68JM) whom Jerry had contacted the year before (see 353—9A2PM). The gear he brought along to this remote location is quite impressive, particularly the Rohn Hbx-48 tower, Mosley Pro 67 yagi, and 1/4 wave verticals stretching up to the sky behind the group in the photo.

357—HF0POL

The Henryk Arctowski Station of the Polish Academy of Sciences carries out biological, meteorological, and geophysical research. Since 1977, a staff of 19 Polish scientists and technicians have been researching year-round on King George Island in the South Shetlands.

358—S21ZG

If everyone in the world were crammed into the continental United States, population density still would not equal that of Bangladesh. Formerly East Pakistan, Bangladesh won its independence in 1971. Since that time amateur radio operation from Bangladesh has been sporadic and the legality of such operations often questioned. That has all changed and amateur radio is now legal in Bangladesh thanks to patient persistence of the local radio enthusiasm the International Amateur Radio Union and help from the ARRL, the International DX Association, Northern California DX Foundation, and companies such as MFJ, Ham Radio Outlet and Moseley Electronics.
—From the card

CZECHOSLOVAKIA BREAKS
IN TWO

VACLAV HAVEL ELECTED AS CZECH
PRESIDENT

Howland Island is a 400 acre, flat coral island 1/2 mile wide and 1 1/2 miles long, located roughly 50 miles north of the equator and 1700 miles southwest of Hawaii. It is uninhabited and vegetated only by grasses, vines, and lowgrowing shrubs due to scant rainfall, constant wind and scorching heat. It was claimed by the US under the Guano Act in 1856 because of the phosphate rich guano deposits which were mined until 1878. As with Jarvis Island (see 295—AH3C/KH5J), the US colonized Howland with young Hawaiian men in the mid- to late-1930s. It was during this time that the first amateur radio operation took place from this location.

Howland Island was to be the destination for Amelia Earhart when she departed New Guinea on her round-the-world flight. She was to land on the hurriedly competed airstrip there. However, she and her navigator Fred Noonan, never arrived. To this day their fate is still debated.

During World War II, Howland served as an American air base as did nearby Baker Island, 40 miles to the south. Since 1974, Howland and Baker Islands have been part of the Pacific/Remote Islands National Wildlife Refuge complex, overseen by the Fish & Wildlife Service of the Department of the Interior.

The AH1A crew of ten operators and two wildlife biologists boarded the 70 foot schooner Machias at Christmas Island, Eastern Kribati for the seven day sail to Howland.

A stay on the island of nine days had been planned, however, it was extended to 15 days due to bad weather brought on by patterns known as El Nino. Howland Island is surrounded by a narrow fringing reef, and access to the island is only over the reef in small landing boats as there is no dock. Rough surf and high seas prevented the team's departure from the island and prevented the support vessel from reliably supplying the team with food, water and fuel. During the final six days on the island, survival techniques of gathering water from giant clamshells and rainwater for drinking was necessary.

...We believe this to be only the second operation from Howland Island since World War II, the first being in 1988. Over 52,000 QSOs were made by the AH1A team.

—From the card

AH1A
HOWLAND ISLAND
1993

359—AH1A 2/1/93 (N:155)

360—5W0CW 2/19/93 (N:155)

361—VP8CMX 3/17/93 (N:156) SEE 299

364—ZK1AT 1/31/94 (N:155)

365—9J2CE 4/11/94 (O:157)

368—EG9A 10/10/95 (M:157)

369—9U/F5FHI 10/18/95 (N:157) SEE 328

WORLD TRADE CENTER BOMBED

RWANDAN GENOCIDE BEGINS;
800,000 SLAUGHTERED

362—OM3EA 10/29/93 (N:157)

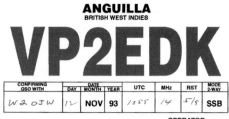

ANGUILLA
BRITISH WEST INDIES

VP2EDK

| CONFIRMING QSO WITH | DATE | | | UTC | MHz | RST | MODE 2-WAY |
	DAY	MONTH	YEAR				
W2OJW	12	NOV	93	1055	14	5/5	SSB

OPERATOR:
DUNCAN KREAMER, ESQ.
W1GAY
73

☐ PSE QSL ☑ TNX QSL   A W4MPY QSL

363—VP2EDK 11/12/93 (H:156)

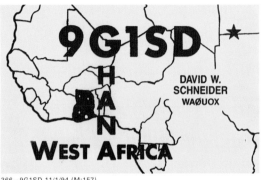

366—9G1SD 11/1/94 (M:157)

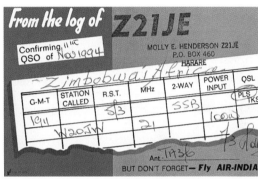

367—Z21JE 11/11/94 (O:157) SEE 164, 224, 273

NELSON MANDELA ELECTED
PRESIDENT OF SOUTH AFRICA

Jerry's QSL collection ends in 1995, but his story didn't.

He continued on the air, usually rising as early as three A.M. to work DX. He remained active in various radio organizations: Jerry was a technical associate of the Society of Wireless Pioneers, a recipient of the 70th anniversary award of the Quarter Century Wireless Association, the fourth president of his chapter, and an "Elmer of the Year."

Jerry's other passion was the trombone. He was a member of the Musicians' Union, and played gigs and marched in parades until he was well into his 80s.

He led an active life for a man of his age. He worked out daily at the Hackensack YMCA, swimming laps in the pool and walking on the treadmill. At age 90, he had surgery to correct his cataracts, and his doctors convinced him to stop his exercise program. When his insurance company insisted he take a physical at 91, he passed with flying colors. And he continued to drive his car until February 27, 2001, when during a visit to his bank he felt ill, went to the hospital, and died peacefully at age 92. His radio license outlived him, expiring on November 2, 2003.

GEORGE W. BUSH
INAUGURATED

JERRY POWELL:
THE LIFE OF A HAM

FIG. 34

Jerry brings his
fiancée Mabel to
meet the family,
circa 1930.

FIG. 35
Jerry, Mabel, and
Donald Powell

FIG. 36
(overleaf)
Chief Engineer
Powell and
Lieutenant Colonel
S. Shiffrin

FIG. 37

(*previous*)
Jerry and co-workers
at Bendix

FIG. 38

(*previous*)
Jerry and his band

FIG. 39

Jerry at a meeting
of the Quarter
Century Wireless
Association

MORSE CODE

Most hams are fairly proficient at Morse code; until recently it was a mandatory part of every licensing exam. Today, the standards have been relaxed for an entry-level license but, for the high-frequency bands from 160 to 10 meters where DXing takes place, Morse code is required.

To the uninitiated, it may seem cumbersome to communicate by spelling out your words in "dits" and "dahs," but code retains a lot of utility, particularly under conditions in which the higher bandwidth of a voice message cannot get through clearly enough to be properly understood.

Another advantage of code is that it can be sent and received with more rudimentary equipment. Even novice hams could build themselves simple equipment that can handle Morse code. The latest commercially available gear has all sorts of filters for narrow and variable bandwidth and electronic code keyers that are capable of recording and playing back multiple messages from memory in case the listener misses the occasional letter here and there.

Hams refer to Morse code transmissions as "CW," or continuous wave. Essentially, the transmitter on their radio is putting out a constant signal, which is interrupted periodically to send code, sort of like flicking on and off a light switch. The pattern of the interruption conveys the message.

Someone receiving such a signal will indicate on his QSL cards whether voice or code was the mode of the signal received. Seasoned CW enthusiasts can transmit code at 20 to 30 words a minute using a rich collection of abbreviations or "Q codes." They are so adept that they needn't write down the messages but can decode the letters in their heads as they hear them.

Hams report hearing codes in the most unlikely places. One told us of overhearing messages through the speakers of the New York subway's announcement system. What sounds like static to most of us is a vivid language to the CW expert.

Hams also set up Morse code networks, or "nets," that allow for multiple conversations simultaneously. Instead of sending a CQ call into the ether, hams can gather and know that they'll have people to contact all gathered together. At a predetermined time, hams sign in to a particular frequency and chat.

FIG. 40-42

Morse code keyers

Samuel Finley Breese Morse (FIG. 43) invented his code in the 1840s (FIG. 45). Its original use was for the transmission of information through electromagnetic pulses via wires or cable. Commercial telegraph companies, railroads, newspapers, businesses, and the military used it to transform the efficiency of their operations. Trains and troop movements could be coordinated, while news and business data could travel as never before.

With the development of Marconi's wireless at the turn of the century, Morse code became airborne. At the outset, its greatest use was for communication with ships at sea. This maritime system soon became the international standard and to this day is considered the best way to communicate with hams not fluent in English.

By the 1960s, radiotelegraphy was on the wane. Railroads and Western Union had phased it out, and today its use is limited to some shore-to-ship communications. Nonetheless, this electronic communications standard that predates the Internet by about 150 years is still alive and flourishing thanks to the amateur radio community.

FIG. 43

Samuel Morse

PHONETICS

Hams' messages are often plagued with static and interference. To clarify their communications, particularly when spelling out their call numbers, they use a phonetic alphabet. Operators in different parts of the world may have their own systems, and some hams make up their own humorous sequences. In the interests of clarity, however, most hams rely on the ITU phonetic alphabett:

FIG. 44

ITU phonetic alphabet

Alpha Bravo Charlie Delta Echo
Foxtrot Golf Hotel India Juliet Kilo
Lima Mike November Oscar Papa
Quebec Romeo Sierra Tango Uniform
Victor Whiskey X-ray Yankee Zulu

MORSE CODE

. dit   - dah

A .-	H	O ---	V ...-	3 ...--
B -...	I ..	P .--.	W .--	4 ....-
C -.-.	J .---	Q --.-	X -..-	5 .....
D -..	K -.-	R .-.	Y -.--	6 -....
E .	L .-..	S ...	Z --..	7 --...
F ..-.	M --	T -	1 .----	8 ---..
G --.	N -.	U ..-	2 ..---	9 ----.
				0 -----

Question ..--..   Comma --..--   Period .-.-.-

A dash time is equal to three times the length of the dot

FIG. 45

Morse code

View from above

FIG. 46

Proper keying position

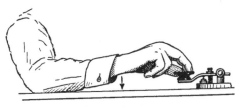

Side view

HAS THE

INTERNET

REPLACED

THE NEED FOR

HAM RADIO?

Ham radio remains vital and alive in the twenty-first century. Every week, the FCC releases a list of the hundreds of newly licensed hams that have passed their exams and are excited about joining the community of more than 600,000 already on the air. For many of them, there is no parallel to the good natured ragchew during the evening commute or the thrill of making a new DX contact with a former stranger on the other side of the Earth. The authors of this book recently passed our own exams and began tentative steps out onto the air. We can report that the warm welcome to a lively community is like nothing we've experienced in a decade on the Internet.

Still, ham radio is far more than a pastime. As we've discussed earlier, it provides a vital community service in times of emergency, a function that can never be replaced by the Internet that is so dependent on phone, cable, and electrical lines, all vulnerable in times of crisis.

To Americans the world seems to be shrinking dramatically—CNN shows us events a half planet away as they unfold—we have internet, email, and mobile phones to link us anywhere. But even though 500,000,000 people are online, most of the places that Jerry contacted are still very inaccessible.

Only 10,000 of the 40,000,000 people in the Sudan and half a percent of Russians are wired. Beyond South Africa, 999 out of 1,000 Africans have never been online. Less than eight percent of people in Tonga even have a telephone. In China, email can still send you to jail.

The majority of the people on earth don't have computers. They don't have electricity. And they have never made a phone call in their lives. Despite a century of telecommunications, in many places ham radio is still a leading edge technology.

ACKNOWLEDGMENTS

Many hams helped us understand this great hobby and learn more about Jerry's collection: Dave Landry, KA1CRP; Leif Lindgren, SMØFWW; Max C. de Henseler, HB9RS; Yan Bambang Susanto, YB3CEV; Bill Booth, VE3AAA; and Jeanne Bard Whitsett.

> Special thanks go to Bob Hopkins, WB2UDC, who helped us avoid mistakes on the air and in print.

Thanks to Donald Powell, who was very generous with his time, memories, and family album.

Thanks to Paul Cassel, VE3SY, for permission to use the Jack Cummings article from the Kitchener-Waterloo Amateur Radio Club History Project. And to Jennifer Hagy at the ARRL for permission to use various images from *QST Magazine*.

Thanks to our friends at Princeton Architectural Press, particularly Deb Wood and our editor, Jennifer Thompson.

Thanks to these graphic designers whose work helped make this book possible: Cara Brower, Rogier Klomp, Josh McDowell, Matthew McGuinness, Heng Wee Tan, Jean Marc Troadec, and Alyce Waxman.

Thanks to Emily Oberman for her opinions, input, and smarts.

Thanks to our many encouraging friends: Bill Abrams, Nicholas Blechman, John Fulbrook, Jason Fulford, Amy Fusselman, Hazel Kahan, Hjalti Karlsson, Richard Mehl, Christoph Niemann, Michael Northrup, David Plunkert, Brian Rea, Pam Rice, Stefan Sagmeister, Julie Salamon, Scott Santoro, Paula Scher, Leanne Shapton, Bonnie Siegler, Arline Simon, David Simpson, Jeremy Soule, Miranda Steiger, Scott Stowell, Cynthia Tsai, Quentin Webb, Jan Wilker, James Victore, and Robert Wong.

We managed to build a virtual time machine by amassing a huge collection of back issues of *QST Magazine,* the official organ of the ARRL, stretching back to the early 1930s. These magazines transported us back to the various stages of Jerry's development, showing us the ham issues of the day in articles, diagrams, and ads. Each month was full of homebrew advice, competition results, personal experiences, as well as opinions, comings and goings, and lists and lists of QSOs. We were struck by how many things haven't changed in the ham world over the past 70 years.

Two Hundred Meters and Down (1936) by Clinton B. DeSoto is the definitive history of early ham radio, written while the details were still fresh. We also found some early novels quite helpful in understanding the passion young people in America felt for "the new fandangle." Two favorites were *The Radio Boys' First Wireless* (1922) by Alan Chapman and *Stand By: The Story of a Boy's Achievement in Radio* (1930) by Hugh McAlister.

The Complete DX'er (1983) by Bob Lochner, W9KNI, is as close as a non-ham is likely to come to having a complete DXing experience. It reads like a transcription of a fascinating monologue, like sitting at an old ham's elbow for a week full of radio sessions, sometimes so jargon-laden it's poetic, but always full of enthusiasm and stories that capture the passion and adventure of ham radio.

All About Ham Radio (1992) by Harry Helms, AA6FM, is the most accessible and useful introduction to the subject we came across.

The ARRL has been putting out publications for most of its history, and we reviewed various incarnations of primers they've published to help novices pass their licensing exams, including: *The Radio Amateur's Handbook,* (1944), *How to Become a Radio Amateur* (1964), *The Radio Amateur's License Manual* (1967, 1969, 1972), and *Now You're Talking* (1991, 2001). These were all useful in understanding the technology but the most official and impersonal of the introductions to the subject.

INTERNET RESOURCES

The Internet augments many hams' on-air activities. Here are some of the major sites that will help you learn more about this fascinating hobby and the people who enjoy it:

AC6V's Amateur Radio and DX Guide: a great hub of information
www.ac6v.com

ARRL: the site of the American Radio Relay League
www.arrl.org

DXing.com: created by Harry Helms, author of our favorite guide
www.dxing.com/index.html

Ham Gallery: a great place to see many more QSL cards
www.hamgallery.com

K1DWU: 4500+ links
www.k1dwu.net

Qrz.com: includes a thorough database of call letters
www.qrz.com/index.html

Qsl.net: one of the largest ham sites
www.qsl.net

AUTHORS' NOTE

Near the end of his life, Jerry Powell gave his son Donald a phone number. It belonged to a dealer in ham gear whom Jerry told his son to call when he died. The dealer took away two truckloads of radios, antennas, odds and ends, and a three-ringed binder full of QSL cards. Some time later this album ended up on a folding table at a flea market where I came upon it. Intrigued, I bought the collection, took it home, and puzzled over it. Eventually I determined it had something to do with ham radio, a topic I knew nothing about. Over the next year, Paul and I both learned a great deal about this hobby. We spoke with dozens of hams around the world, read books, visited hamfests, and eventually got our own licenses. Today we are regulars on repeaters around New York and New Jersey. Though we never met him, Jerry was our Elmer. We hope he does the same for you.

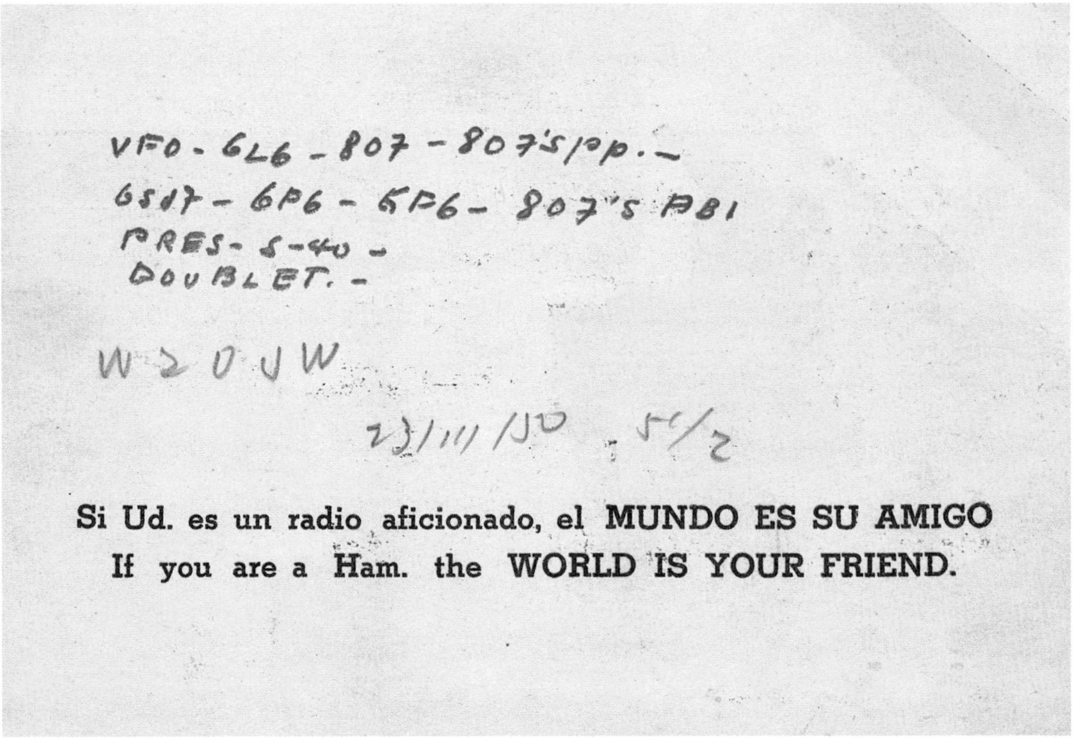

VFO - 6L6 - 807 - 807's/pp. -
6517 - 6P6 - 6P6 - 807's PBI
PRES - S - 40 -
DOUBLET. -

W2DJW

23/11/50 . 5½

Si Ud. es un radio aficionado, el MUNDO ES SU AMIGO
If you are a Ham. the WORLD IS YOUR FRIEND.

113—HK1FE (BACK)